Mysteries and Miracles of New Mexico

By Jack Kutz

RHOMBUS PUBLISHING COMPANY

Rhombus Publishing Company
P.O. 806, Corrales NM 87048

To

LaDonna and Julie,

the two most enchanting

people in my life.

CONTENTS

FOREWORD

New Mexico has always been a strange land, a place where miracles are almost commonplace, a corner of the world where mysteries arise as surely as the moon over the desert.

New Mexico glows beneath an invisible mystic rainbow, shimmers in an aura of enchantment. It draws magic personages from all parts of the universe . . . from across the seas, from across the eons, from the multi-leveled Underworld of Creation and from the stars above.

There is ample reason for calling New Mexico the "Land of Enchantment": its strangeness rarely fails to hold visitors spellbound.

Some of New Mexico's mysteries are fairly well-known. Tens of thousands of people have marveled at the Miraculous Staircase in Santa Fe, or visited the Santuario de Chimayó where miraculous cures have been recorded for more than a hundred years. Yet few people know the beautiful and incredible stories behind these wonders. Other mysteries in this extraordinary land are even less well-known, consisting of tales all too infrequently told. These other stories are in imminent danger of being forgotten, left neglected on the shelves of rarely visited archives, on microfilm seldom unrolled, or in the fading memories of local folk who will not remain with us forever.

That, then, is the reason for this book. It is an attempt to rescue from oblivion aspects of the magical side of New Mexico's history and present them for the first time in a single volume.

Writing this book was often like picking up pottery shards in a desert arroyo. If you find enough of the scattered pieces, you can restore the original pot, re-creating its dazzling design and colors. As I researched facts for the stories in this book, I was surprised to discover that none of the tales had ever been told, in its entirety, by a single source. Even books completely devoted to a specific subject often missed some fascinating details that were available elsewhere. In my research, I would find a tantalizing fragment of a mystery on one side of my literary arroyo, and then dig up a matching piece from another source. Some of the original historians had been quite thorough, while others were inclined to carelessness. No two historical accounts are ever quite identical, just as two eye witnesses to an event can describe it differently. Only by extensive cross-referencing and careful weighing of one set of facts against another can we be sure the true story is emerging.

I have tried to do this throughout this book . . . to gather all the available facts and present all aspects and perspectives of each story. I have tried to respect the views of both the believer and the skeptic. While some readers may find the stories here so bizarre that they lack credibility, it should be understood that other people believe those same tales fervently. While one person's experience may tend to invalidate a particular story, another person's experience may corroborate it.

My approach is to present as accurate a re-creation as possible of the events, lives and situations which, by all accounts, were extraordinary.

In the process, I became indebted to many people. Most of them were already gone before I began my research, but they left a part of themselves in the form of autobiographies, research papers, newspaper columns, magazine articles and rare, obscure books. The people who serve as sources for the information in these pages deserve more than mere footnotes to the history of New Mexico; their efforts should be remembered and appreciated. Other people still living were immensely helpful to me, the ones to whom I had the pleasure of talking. I hope I have given them sufficient credit throughout the text.

As often as possible, I have made use of direct quotes from interviews, court records, public hearing testimony, public domain books and other historical references. In many cases, however, we can never know what people actually said as they reacted to the bizarre events described herein. In such cases, I have taken a certain narrative license to re-create their experiences as historical facts suggested.

As I wrote this book, I would sometimes glance up at a Navajo rug on the wall above my desk. It is a simple rug, just two rows of white, rectangular clouds outlined in black against a grey background. But the rug has a "spirit line" woven through its lower border. The barely noticeable line is there in case a spirit got trapped in the rug during the weaving and needed a way out. Perhaps this book is a similar sort of spirit line, a coarsely woven thread sewn into the tightly stitched tapestry of New Mexico's history. Maybe it will release a few spirits confined far too long.

1

NEW MEXICO'S
MYSTERY ROCK

In the timeless reaches of the desert, only the rocks are eternal. Desert sands constantly shift. Straggling vegetation lives out its brief time and dies. Humans come and go. Even the ageless rivers gnaw at their banks and insist on change.

Only the rocks endure. Yielding slowly to the desert's grinding, they stand haughty and aloof, watching the passage of the centuries. The desert's rocks have seen the lifetime of the land, and in their volcanic hearts they hold the desert's history . . . its past, its secrets.

Surely no rock in the deserts of North America ever held a more tantalizing secret than the legendary Mystery Rock of New Mexico.

Fifteen miles northwest of Los Lunas, in the midst of a scorching wasteland, a rounded mesa known as Hidden Mountain rises above the banks of the Rio Puerco. Its arid slopes stretch up to a dark basalt crown and its sides are cleaved by boulder-strewn arroyos. Part way up one of these gullies lies an ordinary stone . . . ordinary, that is, except for one thing.

Carved into the rock is an inscription so strange it puzzled archaeologists, anthropologists and laypersons for more than a hundred years.

The Mystery Rock is part of a basalt column which appears to have toppled onto its side. At the base of the column, a large smooth-surfaced corner stone bears nine lines of writing: 11 sentences composed of 214 letters. Eighteen different letters make up the individual words of the message. Most are Canaanite-Phoenician characters, though, for a time, some observers thought the text included Hebrew characters as well . . . and a few Russian Cyrillic letters, and at least one Etruscan and one Egyptian character.

The words formed by this linguistic potpourri cross and re-cross the rock in perfectly straight lines, carved deep into the age-old lava.

When the dark "desert varnish" that coats basalt is penetrated, the light-colored inner core of the rock shows through, giving the inscription the appearance of chalk words on a blackboard. It stands out sharp and clear. But what does it say? Why is it there? And who was the engraver?

The Mystery Rock's existence has been an open secret for longer than the living memory of its oldest visitor. Indians, prospectors and ranchers have sat before it and scratched their heads in perplexity. Scientists have trooped up the narrow trail like pilgrims to a

THE NEW MEXICO MYSTERY ROCK. The desperate and haunting story it tells went unread for more than 2,000 years.

Photo by LaDonna Kutz

desert shrine. Photographs have been taken, plaster castings made and dozens of theories advanced.

Is it a hoax? By scratching one hard stone against another, one can quickly determine the time required to make a single deep incision into solid basalt. Cutting the inscription was an incredibly painstaking process. Why would anyone labor long hours in the broiling sun in an obscure arroyo to create a cryptogram which might never be found?

Proponents of the hoax theory have suggested that the work was done by early anthropology students from the University of New Mexico, that the inscription is nothing more than a brilliantly conceived college prank. These skeptics claim the carving is of recent origin and cite as evidence the fact that the eminent archaeologist Adolph Bandelier explored the area in 1880 and made no mention of a mystery stone in his lengthy report.

However, Florencio Chavez, Sr., a former Los Lunas resident, has reported being shown the rock by his maternal grandfather, Simón Serna. Serna was born in 1829 and his father had seen the rock for the first time around 1800. The inscription on the stone is many years older than either Bandelier or the University of New Mexico's first anthropology student.

If not a hoax, then what? A treasure marker, perhaps? Attempts have been made to dig beneath and around the stone. The excavators found nothing but more rock.

How then was the rock's mystery to be solved? The first clue is that the periods come at the beginnings of the sentences. It is obvious that the message must be read from right to left. Many ancient languages are read in this way.

In 1948, William H. McCart, an Albuquerque metallurgist and occasional prospector, took an interest in the rock. He photographed it and sent a photo to Dr. Robert H. Pfeifer of the Semitic Museum at Harvard University. In the February 1949 issue of *Isis* magazine, Pfeifer wrote that upon examination of the photograph, he recognized it as a summary of the Ten Commandments in Hebrew based on *Exodus 20: 2-17:* "I am Yahweh thy god who brought you out of the land of Egypt. ... "

The inscription was, he wrote, an excellent imitation of the old Phoenician alphabet which had not been in use for two millennia. "The discovery of who engraved that inscription in New Mexico would be an interesting item of Americana," he added.

Interesting, indeed ... but it would be nearly 30 more years before that discovery was made.

The Pfeifer translation was generally accepted as the true one and the Mystery Rock was often referred to as The Ten Commandments Rock.

Frank Hibben, professor of anthropology at the University of New Mexico, was one of the first to take a crack at identifying the mysterious engraver. Hibben speculated that Mormons had done the work during one of their early migrations across the state. He felt certain that the inscription was not ancient. He stressed emphatically that it was not Phoenician. It was archaic Hebrew, he said, probably done about 1900. He did not challenge the assertion that the message was the Ten Commandments, but he noted that it was "a little different" than in the Old Testament, and that it followed the *Talmud* instead.

Now the Mormons took an interest in the curious rock. The Archaeological Society of Brigham Young University in Provo, Utah, sent an investigative team to make a study. The Church of the Latter Day Saints felt that "such a discovery would appear to agree with the *Book of Mormon*", but they were concerned that acceptance of the rock as a Mormon artifact could prove embarrassing to the church if it were later shown to be fraudulent.

The Mormon team examined the stone and in 1954, published an article which stated the inscription was quite recent because a mere glance was "enough

to reveal the crisp freshness of the newly cut letters."
The investigators should have taken a little closer
glance, for the "crisp freshness" was due to the fact
that McCart and others had frequently scratched chalk
into the incisions to facilitate photography.

By now, the experts had all completed their examinations of the stone, published their contradictory
findings and gone on to other subjects. It was time now
for the amateurs to take over.

In 1964, an Albuquerque attorney, Robert LaFollette approached the mystery from a new perspective.
By first determining the phonetic sounds for each of
the apparently Phoenician characters, he was able to
read the inscription aloud. Much to his surprise, it
sounded very much like the Navajo language! A quick
check of the federal Bureau of Indian Affairs' Navajo
dictionary confirmed it. LaFollette, with the help of a
Navajo interpreter, translated the rock's message into
English and found it to be a story of an epic journey. It
told of a people pursued by enemies and fleeing across
water. There was an account of a battle and an ordeal
of thirst and hunger. The travelers met other tribes,
were aided by them and at last arrived at a river where
they built their homes.

Now, there were two completely different translations of the same inscription and the LaFollette inter-
pretation again posed more questions than it
answered.

Could there actually be a connection between the
Navajo language and Phoenician? Did Navajos ever use
stone writing in such a sophisticated way? And what of
the Navajos' Athabascan ancestors . . . where are *their*
inscription rocks?

Puzzles seemed to appear within puzzles. The
more the Mystery Rock was studied, the deeper its
mystery grew. Many people have climbed the mesa
above in search of additional clues. From the summit,
a magnificent desert panorama spreads out in all directions. The muddy Rio Puerco follows its tortured,

twisted course through wild, empty country. To the east, the escarpment of the Manzano Mountains near Albuquerque rises sharply; to the west, a maze of tablelands and canyons pile up one behind the other. Scattered over the hump-like crest of Hidden Mountain, the broken ruins of many Indian pithouses are clearly visible along the edge of the mesa, as are dozens of petroglyphs, the Indian rock drawings. There can be no doubt that this desert hill once hosted an Indian village.

The Archaeologist Bandelier sifted through these ruins in 1880. Simón Serna's father was here even earlier. And long, long ago someone else walked on the crest of this hill, here before all the others . . . before the pithouses were built and before the petroglyphs were pecked into the rocks. That earlier visitor left an indelible mark, a sharp, clear message which is enigmatic only because we now poorly understand the language he once wrote so eloquently and precisely.

Who on earth was this ancient writer?

LaFollette claimed that a plaster cast he made of the stone revealed two faintly drawn human faces which, to the naked eye, are indiscernible on the actual rock surface. Could that possibly be true? Or did LaFollette simply have a good imagination? For that matter, Pfeifer and Hibben were not entirely in agreement. What if none of the three of them was correct? So far, there seemed to be no completely satisfactory answer.

Then, one night in the late 1970s, an Albuquerque woman named Dixie L. Perkins sat down to watch a KOB-TV program, "Mysteries of the Desert". There on her television, she got her first glimpse of the Mystery Rock. Immediately she told her husband, "We must go see it." And once she had, she found she could not rest until she had "pulled the secret out of that rock".

Four days later, she had not only done exactly that, but she had also discovered the name and nationality of the engraver!

Dixie Perkins was uniquely qualified to make this incredible breakthrough. For years, she had been actively interested in epigraphy, the fascinating art of deciphering, interpreting and classifying ancient inscriptions. She had made translations of 3,500-year-old cuneiform, and had studied the Greek and Latin languages. She was also a professional calligrapher with 35 years' experience.

Perkins quickly picked up on clues the archaeologists and scholars had apparently missed. She identified the letters as being from the Phoenician-Greek alphabet which was in use in 500 B.C. She noticed at once that all the letters were capitals, a style of printing used exclusively in early Greek. She also discovered that many of the vowels had been left out. But perhaps her most important observation was that the Cypriote Greek letter "S" appears on the stone.

This strange symbol does not resemble a contemporary "S" in any way. It is actually two individual characters... two horizontal "E" balanced on stems and facing each other. The character was in use in the 4th Century B.C.—but was not discovered by scholars until 1910.

The Cypriote Greek "S" was unknown when the Mystery Rock was first visited by contemporary man. The antiquity of the inscription was now firmly established.

Next came the intricate process of translation. Perkins took the letters one by one: the Phoenician "A", which looks like a horned cow skull lying on its side, the "B" which resembles a printed number "9", the "G" like a tilted "7", and so on.

Finally the deciphering required Perkins to supply the omitted vowels, and then to translate the resulting Canaanite-Phoenician-Greek message into English. The words began to emerge.

The first four letters in the upper right hand corner became "ANKM". Using the Greek root words "ANA" and "IKW", and by adding the necessary vowels,

Perkins was able to complete the Greek word "ANI-KNEOMAI". That done, the Mystery Rock began to tell its story: "I have come up to this point, or place. . . . "

About half-way through the text, Perkins translated the word "ZAKNR". With the missing vowels added, it became "ZAKYNEROS", a proper name. "I, Zakyneros, . . . " it read. As the translation unfolded, she learned the author was from the Grecian area of the Mediterranean Sea—and that his story was both extraordinary and haunting.

She first published her translation in 1979. Then, in 1981, she obtained an old photograph of the Mystery Rock taken about 1950. She compared the words in the photograph to the ones she copied directly from the stone in 1978, observing that a few letters had been defaced and even broken off in the interim. Consequently, she re-translated three words in her first version to conform to the meaning of the original words as depicted in the photograph.

With Perkins' permission, her remarkable translation, in its entirety, is as follows:

"I have come to this place to stay. The other one met with an untimely death in battle, dishonored, insulted and stripped of flesh. The men thought him to be an object of care whom I looked after, considered crazed, to be tossed about as if in a wind, to perish in poverty and need. By my kinsmen I was respected and honored, of blessed lot, with a body of slaves and so many olive trees, a peg to hang anything upon. Men punished me with exile to exact retribution for a debt; meanwhile, I remain here as a rabbit. I, Zakyneros, just as a prophet, out of reach of mortal man, I am fleeing and very afraid. I am dross, scum, refuse, just as aboard ship a soft, effeminate sailor is flayed with an animal hide, all who speak offensively are lashed or beaten with a cane; but after a short time, the hurtful ones may be sated; at an unseasonable time, I remain to protect from the rainy southwest winds the

hollow or the ravine. Very much harvest is gathered in, very much is in the woody dell and glen; very many bags of young deer. Very many hides with delicate, luxuriant hair; by the channel of a river, swift flowing. Very much is given by the gods, the choicest kind of gift, to call upon the gods for again and again, at the unseasonable time I become gaunt from hunger."

Zakyneros, speaking from a stone lodged on the side of a desert mesa, immortalized his anguish, leaving us to wonder about his eventual fate.

"It took courage to contradict the Ten Commandments version," said Perkins. "Some people say my translation is bunk because they don't want to believe it isn't the Ten Commandments. But Pfeifer's translation was cursory. A Jewish lady friend of mine, who taught Hebrew in a private school for many years in New York City, did a critique of the Ten Commandments version. She concluded that about 60 percent of that translation was in the translator's mind."

So, now that the puzzle is solved at last, can the Mystery Rock finally be forgotten? Not at all. What Dixie L. Perkins has done is open a door, throw a shaft of light down a previously dark corridor of history. She has proven the Mystery Rock is older than Columbus, older than the Vikings' explorations.

Zakyneros, lonely as he may have been when he died, did not come here alone. He traveled with others, across the Atlantic, and over half an unexplored continent to an obscure river known today as the Rio Puerco. Did his companions build settlements? Did they leave other traces of their passage? If so, can they be found?

Dixie Perkins' solution to the Mystery Rock has simply presented many new mysteries to discover.

HOW TO GET TO THE MYSTERY ROCK

A visit to the Mystery Rock may start by driving west from Albuquerque 28 miles on Interstate Highway 40 to the Los Lunas exit, Number 126. Head south on State Highway 6. Eighteen miles down the state highway, a dirt road leads west, over the railroad tracks, toward Hidden Mountain. The road forks after .7 of a mile. Keep to the left for another half-mile. Here, a narrow, sandy track goes off to the right and ends near a barbed wire fence after .2 of a mile.

Walk to the right along the fence line and watch for a pile of rocks in the arroyo to the left. This cairn marks the beginning of the well-worn, much-used trail that leads to the Mystery Rock. This terrain is very hot in summer. It must be remembered that this is private land and is frequently patrolled; landowner rights must be respected.

BIBLIOGRAPHY

NEW MEXICO'S MYSTERY ROCK
Chapter One

Albuquerque Journal, September 23, 1979.
Albuquerque News, July 30, 1970.
Albuquerque Tribune, February 24, 1972; June 14, 1972.
LaFollette, Robert H., **The Rock that Gives Every Word Wished,** Dallas, Tex., Triangle Publishing Co., 1964.
Perkins, Dixie L., **The Meaning of the New Mexico Mystery Stone,** Albuquerque, N.M., Sun Publishing Company. 1979.
South Valley News, March 2, 1967.
Williams, Brad and Pepper, Choral. **The Mysterious West,** New York. Holt, Rinehart and Winston. 1970.

2

KATZIMO: THE
ENCHANTED MESA

Out in the vast, lonely mesa country west of central New Mexico, a rolling, flowing landscape is punctuated by great islands of rock. One in particular is more eye-catching than the rest. It stands near the roadside of Highway 13, less than three miles northeast of Acoma Pueblo, a sheer-walled, 400-foot tower of superbly wind-sculpted sandstone. At dawn and sundown, it glows with an unearthly radiance.

To the Indians, it is known as Katzimo. To the Spanish, it is Mesa Encantada, and in English, Enchanted Mesa.

Enchanted. Mystic. Haunted. Katzimo is all of these. The legend that gives the place its mysterious character goes far back into the timeless darkness of prehistory. According to the traditions of the Acoma Indians, the Keres people once lived on its broad, flat summit. They farmed the plains below and returned at night to their lofty homes by way of a natural rock ladder up the precipitous walls.

Once, while they worked in their fields, a terrible storm enveloped the mesa. It lashed the tiny pueblo with unbelievable fury. In the village were three women, too ill to work, and a young boy, A-chi-te, who was caring for them. The raging wind and rain crushed the adobe houses and A-chi-te's mother lay injured in the debris. A-chi-te moved her carefully out of the rubble and, against the hurricane force of the storm, he struggled down the rock ladder to run for help.

Suddenly he heard a thunderous roar. He turned to see thousands of tons of rock crashing to the ground. The disastrous downpour had undermined the mesa's sandy base. The rock ladder and the pueblo had fallen.

When the storm subsided, the tribe could only stand by in helpless anguish while the three women trapped above slowly perished of thirst and starvation. After this calamity, the tribe is supposed to have moved to the place they still inhabit, to the top of another great rock, the Peñol of Acoma. It is said that the spirits of the three doomed women forever pace the haunted crest of Katzimo.

The first recorded ascent of Katzimo is found in the folktales of the Acomas. One day, Coyote was given some feathers by the Bluebirds and he flew with them to the top of the mesa. Then the Bluebirds took back their feathers and left Coyote behind. When he tried to descend, he fell to the rocks below.

Surely the legendary Coyote was a direct ancestor of Wile E. Coyote of Roadrunner cartoon fame, for he seems to have been just as indestructible, inventive and accident-prone. Soon, we find him winging his way back to Katzimo, this time using pigeon feathers. Once on top, the Pigeons found they could not stand Coyote's dirty mouth, so they took back their feathers and left him crying. Spider heard him and offered to lower him in his basket. "But as you descend," Spider said, "do not look up or I shall drop you."

Naturally, Coyote blew it, just as Wile E. would have. Halfway down, he raised his head to ask why he wasn't supposed to look up and Spider dropped him.

Other early ascents of Enchanted Mesa must have been equally perilous. Southwest writer Mary Katherine Sedgewick's research led her to report that "when an Acoma youth was being instructed in the kiva into the mysteries of the faith, the last step of his initiatory discipline before giving him full freedom as a man was to blindfold him and send him to the top of the Mesa Encantada for a night's lonely vigil, bearing a jar of water as oblation to the spirits. It was explained that a boy could climb blindfolded where he could not go open-eyed."

Today, ropes, chocks and nylon slings allow the modern rock climber to ascend worse exposures than Mesa Encantada, but the Indians used climbing aides of a different sort. At the back of the large amphitheater, supposedly formed by the great, legendary collapse, foot- and handholds have been carved into the sandstone wall. That they are very old is attested to by the fact that they are eroded and smooth. Without the handholds, the wall would present a contemporary rock climber with an enjoyable "friction-pitch", though not, perhaps, while balancing a jar of water.

Above this section, where the mesa turns vertical, a 30-foot long chimney-like crack appears. In this crack, wooden sticks were placed horizontally to form a ladder. The sticks were removable; between ascents, they could be taken out and hidden.

When the white man came to New Mexico, Katzimo held no enchantment for him. Obviously, nothing material was to be gained by its conquest. It was not until more sensitive and inquisitive men visited this land that interest in the mesa appeared. For them, there was a legend to conquer. Had there really once been a pueblo on top? There was only one way to find out—climb Katzimo.

Adolph Bandelier, the 19th Century archaeologist, viewed the mesa and declared it "one of the imposing cliffs in the Southwest" and noted its summit was "utterly beyond reach". Other historians and archaeologists shared his awe of these fearful cliffs, but the mystery of Katzimo drew them to its heights nonetheless.

In 1883, Charles F. Lummis claimed to have somehow struggled to the top, becoming the first white man to ascend the mesa. He reported no evidence of habitation on top. In 1895, F.W. Hodge, of the Bureau of Ethnology in Washington, D.C., attempted the climb. He first examined the talus at the base of the amphitheater and found many fragments of very ancient pottery. In the bowl above, he discovered the hand- and footholds. Using these, he climbed to the foot of the perpendicular crack, but could go no higher.

Two years later, Professor William Libbey, of Harvard, made the ascent by employing a technique which today's mountaineers would tend to frown upon. Nevertheless, the professor's ingenuity must be admired.

Harper's Weekly, August 28, 1897, reported that the Libbey party arrived equipped with "a small cannon and miles and miles of rope". The cannon was used to fire a ring with a line attached, completely over the mesa. Once a rope was in place on the far side, a sort of bo'sun's chair and pulley were set up and Libbey was lifted up the rock.

He spent only two hours on top and found "not the slightest indication" the mesa had ever been inhabited. Still, the controversy would not rest. The Bureau of Ethnology again sent Hodge to tackle the mesa. This time, near the frustrating crack Hodge discovered the hidden sticks. He had brought a ladder of his own and didn't need the sticks, but the secret of the route was now out. Since then, the ascent has been an easy . . . though somewhat novel . . . climb.

THE FLAKE OF ENCHANTED MESA. A rock climber stands atop this 50-foot rock spire, reaching for the mysterious handholds above.

Photo by Jack Kutz

Hodge and his companions spent the night on top, allowing themselves time for a thorough search. They found many interesting things: a prayer-stick, a shell bracelet, white stone axe blades and both ancient and modern potshards. They also examined a crude stone "monument" made of rock slabs, concluding it was man-made.

Did the Acomas really once inhabit Enchanted Mesa? In 1916, Mrs. Sedgewick wrote " . . . the proofs of human occupation of Katzimo seem well established, but whether permanent or only periodic may perhaps never be known."

In contemporary times, Enchanted Mesa was probably climbed more often by white people than by Indians. The once-fearful crag is now considered one of the easier rock climbs in New Mexico. But there is a far more interesting ascent just around the corner to the east of the traditional route. This climb begins on an elegant and incredibly thin rock flake standing alongside the sheer wall.

The flake rises some 50 feet like an enormous Anasazi spear point, and it is usually climbed by using a mountaineering technique known as the "lay-back". By clutching the edge of the flake with one's hands, stretching out and planting one's feet flat against the face of the cliff, it is possible to inch up to the tip of this verticle slab and then step, very carefully, onto its razor-thin point.

Poised there, a climber can look up and see the continuation of the smooth, soaring sandstone wall leading on to the summit. There is nothing much to cling to from here on; it is all boot tips and fingertips the rest of the way . . . if one dared.

But then, as one looks closer, faint, almost imperceptible hand- and footholds become visible. Someone, a long time ago, carved out a precarious route up that wall, above the flake!

But why? One slip would have meant instant death. Why would anyone stand in those tiny toeholds, so fragilely balanced high above the ground while cautiously chipping out the next step? Without the protection of rope and pitons, who would take that kind of risk?

Could it have been A-chi-te? Could he, in a desperate attempt to reach his doomed mother on the summit, have scaled that awesome cliff?

HOW TO GET TO KATZIMO, THE ENCHANTED MESA

Katzimo is located near the roadside of State Highway 23, less than three miles northeast of Acoma Pueblo. A small picnic area near the base of the rock provides a place for parking and a view of the bowl created by the great collapse. From there, a short hike to the north side of the mesa brings one to the sheer rock flake.

Enjoy the mesa's beauty, but enjoy it only from the ground. Acoma Pueblo no longer permits climbing on Katzimo, for, in addition to being haunted and enchanted, it is also sacred.

BIBLIOGRAPHY

KATZIMO: THE ENCHANTED MESA
Chapter Two

Bullock, Alice. **Living Legends of the Santa Fe Country.** Denver, Colo. Green Mountain Press. 1970.

Crenshaw, Jene M. *Summit Magazine,* June, 1972.

Dobie, J. Frank, Boatwright, Mody C. and Ransom, Harry H. **Coyote Wisdom.** Austin, Tex. Texas Folklore Society Publication. 1938.

Lummis, C.F. **A New Mexico David,** New York. Schribner's Sons. 1891.

Peck, Leigh. **Don Coyote.** Boston, Mass. Houghton Mifflin. 1942.

Ungnade, Herbert E. **Guide to the New Mexico Mountains.** Denver, Colo. Sage Books. 1965.

Whiting, Lillian. **Land of Enchantment.** Albuquerque, N.M. Sun Publishing. 1981.

3

SEARCH FOR THE LOST
ADAMS DIGGINGS

"More dead than alive." That's how everyone described the two lurching scarecrows who staggered into Fort Wingate on that hot August afternoon in 1864.

Both men were barely able to stand, let alone walk, and at first, townsfolk stepped out of their way and stared as the strangers stumbled down the dusty streets of the company town. Their clothes were dirty, shredded rags; their feet oozed blood inside their worn-out boots. Their faces were burned raw by the torturing sun. The eyes were glassy and haunted, as if they had stared too long into the fires of hell. When they tried to talk, no words came from their dry mouths.

After they had been given water, they were eased down onto straw-filled pallets. With cool wet rags soothing their foreheads, they fell into restless, feverish sleep.

"That old one won't last much longer," the post doctor said. "But the younger one, he might pull through."

The doctor was right. The oldest died of heat stroke; the other slowly recovered. When he was able to think coherently, he dug frantically in his pants pocket and pulled out a gold nugget the size of a hen's egg. He clenched it tightly as he blurted out a story—a tale so fantastic it would become a legend that would drive men by the hundreds out into the wasteland from which he had just come.

Some of these later men would grow rich and some would lose everything they had. Others would wander for decades, obsessed by the bonanza they could never find. Some would go raving mad, and many of them would die in the search.

The survivor of the pair that crawled into Fort Wingate in 1864 said his name was Adams. That was all, just Adams. His partner's name was Davidson, and that was all that could be put on his tombstone when the townspeople laid him to rest.

Adams' story began in Tucson, Arizona. He was a freighter by trade and had drifted into that town with his 12-horse pack train seeking work. In the local saloons, he met other men who, like himself, were down on their luck. They were mostly out-of-work miners, a few unemployed cowboys and a couple of shaggy old prospectors. When Adams' new friends learned that he spoke Spanish fairly well, they asked him to interpret for them while they talked to another drifter who had also just come into town.

Folks were curious about that particular newcomer. He was obviously a Mexican, yet he spoke Apache as well as Spanish. He seemed to have a message he was trying to convey, but the English-speaking Arizonans could only understand one word he said. It was the only Spanish word they knew, and it was the only word that really mattered to them.

"*Oro.*"

So, that mid-summer day in Tucson, Adams and 12 other men sat down with the Mexican in the shade behind a saloon and listened to his tale.

The man said he had been kidnapped by Apaches when he was a child. He had been raised by the Indians, had grown into manhood in Apachería and had ridden with the Apaches on their journeys and raids. He had become an Indian, yet deep inside, he still longed for his homeland, for his original family. One night, he said, he slipped away from his Apache community and began his long journey back to Sonora, Mexico.

Leaving his Indian life behind him, he found himself entering a bewilderingly different world, where people held values completely alien to those by which he had been raised. It did not take him long to learn that in the society of the non-Indian, one thing was valued more than anything else in life. Although he could not fully understand why these people were willing to kill and die for pretty colored rocks, he knew he could benefit from their strange greed.

The Mexican told his attentive listeners, through Adams, that he knew of a place, far away, where there was so much gold that no horse could carry all the nuggets a man could pick up in a single day, a place where golden flecks swirled in the stream and could be scooped up by the handful.

But the man said his own real goal was simply to return to his family in Mexico. To go home, he needed two horses, a saddle, a rifle, ammunition and $50 cash. If Adams and the other listeners behind the saloon were willing to provide those, the man said he would guide them to the secret canyon deep in Apachería, to a hidden ravine through which he had traveled many times in the past.

Adams and his cohorts eagerly agreed to the bargain. They pooled their money to buy provisions. Adams supplied the horses, and within a week, they were on their way. The Mexican led the expedition due east, out of Arizona and into New Mexico. Where they went from there is a question that would drive other searchers crazy for many, many years to come.

The best bet is that they curved around the northern foothills of what is now the Gila Wilderness, passed along the northeastern tip of the San Augustín Plains and dipped down into the Magdalenas. But, of course, no one will ever know for sure.

At last, the weary expedition's guide took them to the top of a broad mountain ridge and pointed out two sharp, twin peaks on the horizon. He urged them to remember those landmarks. Then he took them deep into a wild, trailless network of canyons that defied human memory. The Mexican halted his horse in front of a second landmark, one that Adams would find extremely hard to describe in later years. He said it looked like the face of a woman painted on the side of a mountain.

Still the party rode on. Finally they reached what seemed to be a sheer, blank wall that blocked all further passage. His followers watched in amazement as the Mexican reined his horse right up to the cliff and disappeared into it.

Apprehensively, the others followed him and found that he had ridden behind an enormous boulder that must have fallen thousands of years earlier, neatly concealing the entrance to a deep, narrow canyon.

The canyon zig-zagged up through the heart of the cliff. It was almost too steep for the horses to climb, and its walls were so close the riders could sometimes extend their arms and touch both sides. There was only a thin rivulet of water in the ravine that time of year, but high above the horsemen were remnants of torrential flash floods. Tree branches, great hunks of grass and even logs had been snagged on the rocks by the fury of the deluges that had often roared like tidal waves through this spooky little gorge where no other white men had ever set foot.

After several sharp twists, the canyon opened up and leveled out for a ways. For a short distance it was broad and sandy. Thick green grass grew around crystal clear pools fed by a light, thin stream sparkling down from the forested crestline above. Adams and his partners quickly dismounted, dropped down on all fours and began grabbing up fistsfull of sand. Adams plunged his arm into one of the pristine pools and pulled out a handful of pebbles. He held them close to his face, peered intently and then let out a joyful whoop that must have echoed for miles.

By now, the others were starting to shout and holler, slapping one another with their hats. They hugged the Mexican and pounded his back. Everything was just as he'd said it would be. He had led them to the biggest paystreak this side of California!

The exuberant prospectors gladly gave the Mexican everything they had promised and as a parting gesture, Adams took off his favorite red bandana, tied it around the Mexican's neck and gave him a final *abrazo*. Shortly after dark, the Mexican rode off on his long journey back to Sonora. He had gained very little in the bargain he had made, but, ironically, he turned out to be the only lucky one in the bunch.

Adams and his friends went to work at dawn the next morning. Some of them started panning while others nailed together a crude rocker and a sluice box. By noon, they realized they would be able to produce a least a thousand dollars worth of washings a day... easily.

In the Apache Nation of 1864, nothing went unnoticed for very long. Less than 24 hours later, a heavily-armed band of Indians rode down from the hillside and demanded to know what the intruders were doing on their land. Adams, translating as best he could, explained they were just passing through, picking up a few minerals, and would soon be on their way.

Naturally, the Apaches were suspicious. But they agreed to allow the mining party to stay, under certain strict conditions. They were not to go beyond their current campsite because there was an Apache village in the forest above, and the Indians made it clear that the miners were not exactly honored guests. Their visit was to be a very temporary one.

The miners accepted the Apaches' terms and went back to work. Day by day, their pile of canvas ore sacks grew fatter. Soon, they got tired of sleeping on the ground and started building a cabin. Their supplies were running low, so they sent out a provisioning party.

Then one day, a young and impulsive member of the crew threw caution to the wind and climbed the hill behind their camp. He swaggered back later with a grin on his face and a lump of gold in his hand. "We're scratchin' in chicken feed down here," he said gleefully. "The Mother Lode's up there. The rocks are full of nuggets, bigger'n this one."

Adams grabbed the kid by his shirt. "You damned fool!" he shouted. "Do you want to get us all killed? Hide that nugget under that rock over there and hope to God no Apache saw you take it!"

Next morning, on the day the supply party was due to return, the miners were laboring in the sun when they heard a distant barrage of gunfire. Adams tossed aside his shovel. "Get your guns, boys," he said. "Be on the ready. C'mon, Davidson, let's find out what happened down there."

The two men clattered down the stony ravine and when they raced out from behind the great boulder, they nearly stumbled over the bodies of the four men who had been sent out for beans and flour.

As they knelt beside the corpses of their friends, a second burst of gunfire erupted at the top of the canyon. Quickly, they dove into the brush; after the shooting stopped, they watched a plume of smoke rise from the spot where their cabin was located.

Adams shook his head and Davidson crossed himself. After dark, they crept stealthily back up the ravine.

Their worst fears were realized when they entered camp. The Apaches had clearly re-established their land rights; the entire mining party was dead, the cabin was a pile of red-hot coals and the gold, hidden under the hearthstone, was melted beyond recovery.

"We've got to get out of here before daybreak," Adams whispered,"Or we're dead men, too." The two ex-miners backtracked into the canyon. But Adams paused. "Wait," he said. He scuttled back to the large rock, overturned it and dug up the gold nugget beneath. "All right," he rasped, "let's get out of here."

They scurried away in the darkness and raced toward the open land beyond the mountains. All night long they ran, stumbled and fell, got up and ran again. By dawn, they were far from the diggings . . . and hopelessly lost. For the next two weeks, they wandered desperately, trying to hide and travel at the same time. They had no food and rarely found water. On their 13th day, they hit a road and although they didn't know where it led, they followed it. Had Fort Wingate been one day farther down the road, the two wouldn't have survived to create the legend of the Lost Adams Diggings.

Though Davidson rested in a Fort Wingate grave, Adams grew restless to get back to the Apache gold. He had no horses or equipment, but there were plenty of local men more than willing to outfit him. Before long, he was riding at the head of a well-provisioned, well-armed expedition. They rode out proudly, and returned several weeks later in drooping dejection. Adams, they all agreed, had a lot of grit, the tenacity of a bulldog, and a lousy memory.

Adams could not locate even one of his landmarks; half the time, he didn't seem to know what part of the country he was in. His backers left him in disgust, but a new set of investors lined up, money in hand, to finance a second try. The dream was just too big to disbelieve.

After Adams' next expedition also ended in failure, with his compadres threatening to hang him for incompetence, he decided it was time to move on to California where he would tell his tale in the saloons of San Francisco. Adams died in frustrated, alcoholic obscurity.

Meanwhile, back in New Mexico, scores of other men continued the search on their own. Like the Adams expeditions, they, too, found nothing. Except, perhaps, for a German immigrant named Jake Schaeffer.

In 1872, Schaeffer showed up at Fort Craig, carrying a very heavy knapsack. He had gotten lost on a hunting trip, he said, and spent several weeks roaming in the wild, uninhabited country. He estimated he might have covered a couple of hundred miles in his effort to return to civilization.

Once, while searching for water, he discovered a narrow canyon and in its upper reaches, he had stumbled onto *"ein ungeheuerlich Wand"* of gold. He chipped out all the nuggets he could possibly carry and staggered off like a pack mule until he finally reached the safety of Fort Craig.

Once Schaeffer had converted his nuggets to greenbacks, he had no desire to return for more, but he was quite willing to try to tell others the way. Unfortunately, his memory was no better than Adams'. Nothing he said made much sense to the intent group of listeners who were trying to draw mental maps from his words ... until he mentioned the mountain that bore the painted face of a woman.

One man in the crowd raised an eyebrow. He was a grizzled, old frontiersman known as Jason Baxter. He nudged his partner and they walked outside, away from the others. "I know where that mountain is," Baxter confided. "Will you be ready to ride in the mornin'?"

Baxter knew the New Mexico backcountry almost as well as the Apaches did. He had traveled far and wide, hunting and prospecting. He clearly remembered having once seen a rock outcropping which, when viewed from just the right angle, resembled the profile of a woman. Pine trees grew around her face, framing it as if with a head of hair. Traces of copper ore in the rock had stained it like paint, depicting her features. While other men were still arguing over which mountain range to search, Baxter knew exactly where to go.

After a fortnight of travel, Baxter and partner John Poland arrived at the base of a rocky crag. Baxter pointed at the colorful natural portrait high up on a cliff. "Purtier'n the Mona Lisa, ain't she?" he chuckled. He then removed the halter from his mule and turned the animal loose. He had deliberately denied the beast water for two days, and now, the thirsty critter instinctively clopped off toward the only running stream within miles. Baxter and Poland galloped along behind, and in less than an hour, they watched as the mule disappeared behind the giant boulder. The old prospectors burst into laughter, slapped their knees and danced a merry jig. Then they quickly followed the mule.

In the clearing above the narrow part of the gorge, they found the charred remains of a cabin. One careful look at the sand on the canyon floor was enough to make them absolutely sure they were in the right place.

"We'll go to work tomorrow," Baxter said, "But right now, we better git under an overhang. Looks like it's fixin' to rain."

And rain it did. The shower turned into a cloudburst and the shallow stream began to deepen. As the water surged higher, the horses and mule panicked, pulling up their tether-stakes before running off. Above the roar of the storm, Baxter shouted in Poland's ear. "Say one of your prayers, old timer! And let's git the hell outa' here!"

They plunged into the now waist-deep water and struggled against the current at the top of the plunging waterfall in the ravine. Then suddenly, the stalwart old mule swam by, fighting its way past them, heading upstream. The two old men grabbed the animal's neck and it dragged them from the maelstrom onto the hillside. They dropped exhausted onto solid ground.

By morning the storm had passed. The sky was clear, but for Baxter and Poland it was a gloomy day, indeed. Without supplies, equipment or horses, their venture was over before it began. Baxter shrugged and clamped his soggy hat on his head. "We'll just come back another time," he said. They trudged back to Fort Craig.

A couple of years passed before they could get properly outfitted again. Finally the two old prospectors managed to hit the trail once more. This time, they were accompanied by James A. McKenna, a man who would later become a noted author and lecturer. McKenna's tough old companions had no trouble locating the hidden canyon, but when they got there, they found themselves facing a totally new disaster.

The canyon was sealed, completely closed by rocks, dried mud and debris. Apparently many flash floods even worse that the one they survived eventually filled in the narrow gorge. The hillside above had collapsed, bringing down tons of boulders and decomposed granite which now filled the canyon to the brim. The prospectors had made another long journey for nothing.

The Lost Adams Diggings were now doubly lost. Baxter, Poland and McKenna thought there was no point in leading others to the canyon, and without these men as guides, the site was as hard to find as ever.

Still, there were plenty of men who refused to believe Baxter's story that the digging now lay under tons of rock and sediment. Some swore that if they could only find the canyon, they would dig down to the gold.

In the early 1880s, a young man turned up in Silver City carrying a sack of nuggets that he claimed came from a ledge in the Lost Adams Diggings. He said he was going back to his hometown in St. Louis to set himself up in business.

Many other prospectors wasted substantial portions of their lives in pursuit of a golden mirage that might be just over the next hill. A man remembered only as "Pettibone" announced his intention to spend one year seeking the Adams Digging. He quit his job with the Santa Fe Railroad, and roamed the mountains for the next two decades. Michael "Captain" Cooney, a former Territorial legislator, set out on the same quest in 1892; it ended only when he died in 1914. Bob Lewis, one of Adams' original backers, set the all-time record; he spent 30 years of his life looking in all the wrong places.

In 1934, George Fitzpatrick, who was then a columnist for the *Albuquerque Tribune*, related a tale told to him by Azeethin-Benah-Uthin, a Navajo medicine man. The aged Indian said that in 1910, a white man known only as Red Shirt lived with his Navajo wife in Toadalena, northwest of Gallup. Red Shirt would periodically leave his farm and be gone for weeks. When he returned, his saddlebags were filled with gold nuggets. Hauling his strike to Santa Fe, Red Shirt would return home with a wagonload of supplies and lavish gifts for his wife.

But local Navajos, suspecting he was stealing gold from tribal lands, confronted him, demanding that he show them his mine. When Red Shirt refused, there was a fight and he was shot. He died, taking his secret with him.

Were Red Shirt's nuggets from the Lost Adams Diggings? Azeethin-Benah-Uthin seemed to think so.

Could there really be a huge gold deposit out there somewhere that has evaded discovery all these years? New Mexico has been throughly explored and there are almost no totally secret places left. On the other hand, maybe many of us have gone for backcountry hikes and walked right past the diggings.

HOW TO GET TO THE LOST ADAMS DIGGINGS

*By triangulating the points to which persons re-
turning from Lost Adams Diggings have reached, it
can be deduced that the bonanza lies buried in a now-
filled gorge in southwestern New Mexico, probably between Fort Wingate, Fort Craig and Silver City. Many
observers in New Mexico's backcountry have made
landmarks of rock formations resembling a woman's
head. One of the most frequently noted such landmarks in that area is located southeast of Grants, on
the eastern edge of the El Malpais National Monument. But surely the massive black lava flows of the
Malpais would have figured in directions to the Lost
Adams Diggings had that face in the rocks been the
key to its discovery.*

BIBLIOGRAPHY

SEARCH FOR THE LOST ADAMS DIGGINGS
Chapter Three

Albuquerque Tribune. April 10, 11, 1934.
Busher, Jimmie. **Lost Mines and Treasures of the
    Great Southwest.** Berkeley. University of Califor-
    nia Press. 1977.
Dobie, J. Frank. **Apache Gold and Yaqui Silver.** Bos-
    ton. Little, Brown and Company. 1939.
Kay, Eleanor. "Lost Mines and Buried Gold", *New Mex-
    ico Magazine.* September 1935.
McKenna, James. **Black Range Tales.** New York. Bal-
    lantine Books. 1974.
Mitchell, John D. **Lost Mines and Buried Treasures
    of the Great Southwest.** Glorieta, N.M. Rio
    Grande Press. 1970.

4

THE FLIGHT OF THE STONE LION

High on the broad, flat crest of a steep-walled mesa near Bandelier National Monument there is a massive stone lion.

It has crouched there for centuries, its long, out-stretched paws clutching the great volcanic slab from which it was carved. It basked in the summer sun and slept under blankets of winter snow for countless seasons. Ravens had circled it, rattlers had coiled in its shade. Many generations of ancient people had evidently made the difficult ascent up to the piled rock shrine that surrounded the lion.

They had given it turquoise and prayers, asking it to work its special magic.

Standing beside the stone lion are two tall, upright rocks, phallic erections pointed at the sky. Most contemporary anthropologists believe the lion and the megaliths were part of a fertility ritual where Indian women once prayed for the blessings of motherhood.

The lion weighs an estimated 1,000 pounds, and is one of only three bas-relief carvings known to have been created by North American Indians in prehistoric times. The other two are also mountain lions lying side by side within the boundaries of Bandelier National Monument, not far from the park's Painted Cave.

No one will ever know who the ancient sculptor was, nor why this third lion was sculpted on top of a mesa. The dark, blue-green hills of Jemez country rise protectively beyond the lion's mesa, obscuring it and blending it into a larger, broader landscape. From a distance, it is hard to point out the specific mesa guarded by the lion. Aside from the sculpted lion, it seemed there was never anything special about that particular mesa. And even that distinction was lost when, on March 7, 1970, the stone lion flew away.

On that day, a team from the University of New Mexico Anthropology Department and the Albuquerque Mountain Rescue Council scaled the mesa to haul the stone lion from his abode. Scholars and preservationists were concerned that the ages were wearing away at the extremely rare sculpture, exposed as it was to the elements on the mesa top. And worse yet, vandals had found it and had begun chipping away at it. Already, its toes had been deliberately chopped off and all of the turquoise hidden in the treasure hole beneath it had been stolen.

The university anthropologists thought the safest place for this priceless artifact was the Maxwell Museum on their campus in downtown Albuquerque.

Mindful of protocol and property rights, they had consulted with the tribal council for nearby Cochiti Pueblo and obtained permission to relocate the shrine.

What they hadn't sought or obtained, however, was the approval of the magical cat itself.

On that bright, crisp March morning, three members of the Mountain Rescue Council and six anthropologists and university students set off in jeeps to capture the ageless mountain lion for a museum.

Beyond the cheerful apple farms of Dixon, the land is rough and inhospitable. Scraggly junipers raked the expedition's vehicles; rocks battered the under-carriages as the riders tumbled around inside, choking on the dust and clenching their teeth when they slammed across arroyos.

About mid-morning, they finally reached the base of the mesa. And the sun went out.

Clambering out of the jeeps, the crew was beset with foreboding. Shading their eyes, they blinked and squinted, trying to take furtive glances at the black shadow creeping across the face of the sun. Some in the party had known that a solar eclipse was expected, but had forgotten about it until that moment. As they stood in the sudden twilight, they turned their eyes to the mesa and wondered, "Why today? Why did the sun go black just when we got here? Maybe the lion knows we're coming and is marshalling its powers."

When the shadow passed over the sun and the brilliance of its light shone strong once more, such thoughts seemed foolish.

The equipment needed for abducting the stone lion was unloaded and slung onto shoulders ... ropes, parachute shrouds, iron pipes, a steel bar, an old mattress, some climbing carabiners and nylon slings. The hill was steep and rocky; the climbers slipped and sweated as they lugged the paraphernalia up the crumbling slope.

Suddenly, a boulder overturned beneath Anthropologist Elmer "Swede" Scholer. He fell headlong down the slope. The boulder pursued him, caught up and mashed his leg as it bounded on past. Blood was spurting from his punctured calf when the others reached the ill-fated team member.

Again, the strange uneasiness crawled through the minds of the now more hesitant party come to "rescue" the stone lion. "The lion *does* know we're coming," they thought, "and it's doing all it can to stop us."

A quick compress with direct pressure on the injury shut off the flow of blood. Fellow anthropologists helped Swede hobble down to his jeep. One of his students offered to drive him back to town. He consented, but only after being assured the others would continue the salvage mission.

Stone Lion Mesa is capped by sheer volcanic walls embedded with fist-sized chunks of obsidian... the biggest "Apache tears" the climbers had ever seen. Preparing for the final ascent up the walls, they dropped the burdens at the base, found a narrow passageway up the cliff, and scrambled on up to the crest. Ropes were cast down to haul up the gear. On top, the mattress, ropes, shrouds and other equipment were shouldered once more before trekking off to the shrine.

There, in the center of the mesa, they got their first look at the stone lion.

The creature was sunning itself in leonine repose, its head resting between its paws. It was an old shrine, no doubt about that. The lion's features were weathered and smooth. On its face, only the eyes were still distinct... perhaps because the domain it surveyed was one of extreme beauty.

From the throne-like mesa, the lion's view commanded a vast terrain of endless hills. Below, the Rio Grande and Rio Santa Fe carved their canyons, revealing glimmers of dark green water and rocky shorelines. Beyond these hills, far to the northeast, the snow-clad peaks of the Pecos Mountains rise; above that, only the flawless New Mexican sky.

Surely the ancient lion must have loved the sky

best. There were hawks drifting in graceful circles above; later the air would be filled with the haunting cries of high-flying cranes. In summer, there would be thunderheads and rain, but mostly, there would be the sun . . . hot, pure, soothing. The lion was warm to the touch, like the coat of a black cat perched in a windowsill.

Quickly, the team set to work. The "treasure hole", where ritual gifts were left under the shrine, allowed the rescuers to pass ropes under the lion's body. Then a fulcrum was built of stacked rocks, and a long, iron pipe reinforced by a steel bar served as a lever. By sticking the pipe into the ropes and prying against the tottering fulcrum, it was possible to raise the half-ton cat a few inches. While the scholars held their breath, the Mountain Rescue members stuffed the mattress and parachute shrouds under the rock and gently eased it back down.

Everyone . . . except the lion . . . breathed a sigh of relief. So far, nothing had broken and now it seemed the stone lion's fate was sealed. It would not gaze upon the New Mexico sky again for a long, long time. The shrouds were thrown over it; the ageless hills the lion had surveyed for centuries suddenly disappeared in a flash of white canvass. Ropes were cinched down, knots tied, and soon, the lion resembled nothing more than a parcel, perhaps an overweight Egyptian mummy.

The rest of the operation was up to a 20th Century innovation that the Indian artisan who created the feline masterpiece would never have imagined: a helicopter.

The university had rented a helicopter for one hour, just enough time to airlift the lion off the mesa and deposit it on the bed of a three-quarter ton flatbed truck now stationed near a paved road, four air-miles away.

In a sense, it seemed as if this might be a proper way to end the lion's long reign. Perhaps its being snatched up and carried away by a giant bird would ful-

fill some ancient prophecy. If so, the prophecy must
have been considerably more complex, as events would
unfold.

With only an hour's rental, the helicopter lift
would have to go like clockwork. While final riggings
were being secured, two team members scrambled
down from the mesa top to drive back to Albuquerque
to meet the pilot and guide him to the shrine. The ren-
dezvous with the pilot was set for 4:00 p.m. sharp.

At 3:45, the two Mountain Rescue volunteeers
were rolling confidently down the freeway headed for
the airport. At 3:46, they ran out of gas.

Slowly the jeep coasted to a stop on the edge of
four lanes of roaring traffic. The driver banged on the
steering wheel. "What's wrong with the gas gauge? If
the lion caused this, it's smarter than we thought," he
said, only half in jest. Dressed in their mountaineering
costumes, complete with holstered piton hammers,
heavy boots, gaiters and parkas with leather rappel-
patches, the two stranded climbers tried in vain to
hitch a ride on in to Albuquerque. Their strange ap-
pearances seemed to eliminate any chance of being
picked up by a sympathetic motorist. Cars just
swerved a little wider as they streamed past.

Finally, a battered psychedelic Volkswagen from
the Taos Hog Farm commune pulled over and offered a
ride. The occupants were somewhat blissed out, but
not spacey enough to buy the climbers' story about
needing to rent a helicopter to fly into the mountains
to pick up a stone lion. Still, they dropped the hitch-
hikers off at Coronado Airport at 4:02.

Minutes later, they were airborne, racing the helicopter's shadow back to the mesa. With the chopper
thrashing violently to hang in the air above the shrine,
a rope was lowered and secured to the well-packaged
lion. The lion was now firmly in the grip of the me-
chanical bird. As the rope drew taut, and the bindings
stretched, it seemed the centuries-old lion were fighting to remain. Then, it seemed to relinquish. After a

moment's hesitation, when the stone lion floated inside its white wrappings, the helicopter veered away, hauling its suspended cargo inexorably toward captivity in an alien environment.

Speeding through the mesa lands, the silver helicopter appeared to be dangling an enormous white pendant. The chopper covered the four miles to the flatbed in minutes. As it began its slow descent, it whipped the crew below, ready to guide the transfer. Poised to help lower the cargo into place, the crew members were blasted by dirt and gravel swept up by the giant propellor blades.

The ground crew tried to wave signals to the pilot, but they were standing too close to the craft to be seen. Having lost visual contact, the pilot began to lose control of his priceless cargo. The lion was swinging furiously back and forth, uncontrollably. It slammed into the flatbed, smashing out the tail lights and bucked the rear wheels off the ground. The helicopter pulled back, swerved away, circled and came in for another try.

This time the anthropology students directing the transfer stood further back, gesturing wildly to the pilot. Finally the lion was hovering almost where they wanted it placed, almost within reach. A member of the rescue team jumped up onto the flatbed, and, bracing himself against the battering wind, leaned out to grab the rigging. He tugged the huge package closer, but suddenly the pilot prematurely triggered the release mechanism and the lion fell at the climber's feet with a truck-rocking thud, missing his toes by inches.

The helicopter swooped away, leaving the anthropologists and climbers to complete the abduction. Team members gathered around to probe the thick padding for any sign of breakage. When it was at least tentatively confirmed that the lion was intact, they relaxed and sat cross-legged beside the shrine. The same odd feeling crept over them, just as when the sky darkened ominously just before their assault on the lion's mesa refuge.

"You old devil," said the climber whose toes were almost claimed by the cat. "You damn near got me during that split-second over the truck. For one airborne instant, you were free again, and you took a swing at me and missed."

"Don't you think it's time you made peace with us?" one of the anthropologists asked. "We're doing this for your own good, you know." He poked his hand under the padding again; the stone beneath felt cold, disturbingly different from when he had first touched it basking in the sun.

Dusk settled over the land as the rescuers drove their precious cargo carefully back to Albuquerque. The sun went down in a blaze of color, firing clouds as it sunk from sight. Soon, bright city lights sparkled around the truck as it lumbered into town; the neon glitter of an Albuquerque Saturday night broke the spell of the stone lion.

With a strange mixture of sadness and accomplishment, the anthropologists and rescue team members parked the truck behind a chain-link fence at the university, and watched the security guard close and lock the gate. With the lion now a blue-shadowed, white lump under the yard lights, the team began to feel an emotion akin to guilt. The lion looked pretty forlorn now, cheapened and degraded.

But at least it was safe. In its new home, the weather would no longer wear away at it, and the mindless vandals wouldn't chip and deface it. True, the wind would never again caress it and electric lights would have to substitute for the sun. . . .

Once on display in the museum, many visitors would come to see it and, perhaps, something ancient and anthropomorphic would stir briefly within the viewers, much as it had in the rescuers on that strange day in March 1970.

In fact, it didn't work out that way.

A few days after its arrival at the university, the lion, still trussed in the same old mattress and nylon slings, was moved to a corner of the patio at the Maxwell Museum. It was destined to wear that ignominious shroud for many years to come.

When word of the stone's removal got out, the people of San Felipe Pueblo grew very angry. They contended the lion was theirs, not the property of Cochiti Pueblo, and they were offended that they had not even been consulted about the rescue effort. Even at Cochiti Pueblo, many people had been unaware of the tribal council's approval for the stone lion to be taken away, and they were equally upset. Soon both Pueblos demanded that the artifact be returned.

A stalemate ensued when the university maintained that its action had been appropriate since the physical protection of the stone was paramount.

An act of Congress eventually led to a resolution of the impasse. The Native American Religious Freedom Act guaranteed the Indians' rights to protect their shrines. In 1981, the stone lion was returned to its original shrine. The indomitable lion took its second helicopter ride, this time to replace it on exactly the same spot over its now meaningless treasure hole. It was, at last, unwrapped under the beautiful, blue New Mexico sky.

Still, threats to the stone lion continue. Irreverent vandals with hunting rifles, shooting the lion for laughs, or idiotic spray painters may continue their sacrilege. Today, the creature's best protection lies in its obscurity. Pueblo officials, the university professors and others who care about preserving the sculpture, all agree that the fewer people who know its whereabouts the better.

If vandals found it before, they'll no doubt find it again. The aged lion's days may well be numbered, but at least it is back where it wanted to be, in the place it never wanted to leave, basking in the sun, surveying its kingdom, radiating its magic.

Maybe, just maybe, the stone lion has enough magic to look after itself after all. It may be that the magnificent creature will guard its mesa top long after the rest of us are faint memories.

HOW TO GET TO THE STONE LION'S COUSINS

Although the stone lion's shrine must remain a secret place, it is nonetheless possible to visit the other two stone lions which are in the protective custody of the U.S. National Park Service, deep within Bandelier National Monument.

Begin by driving 32 miles south from Española on State Highway 30 to the Bandelier Monument headquarters. It used to be possible to reach the Park Service's stone lions by hiking north from Cochiti-Frijoles Trail along the Rio Grande, but this trail has been so badly damaged by the rise and ebb of Cochiti Lake Reservoir that this path virtually no longer exists.

Nowadays, you must take the Frijoles-Stone Lions Shrine Trail which goes northwest from the monument headquarters for 4.5 miles before it turns southwest and enters Alamo Canyon. One mile later, the trail emerges from the canyon and heads southeast for the last 1.5 miles to the Stone Lions Shrine.

Due to the up-and-down nature of the terrain, this hike is an arduous trek, so be prepared for a good workout.

BIBLIOGRAPHY

THE FLIGHT OF THE STONE LION
Chapter Four

Based on personal experience.

5

THE BLESSED EARTH
OF CHIMAYO

They come to this holy place from far and wide. From across the land come the sick, the lame and the weary pilgrims. Supported by crutches or on the arms of loved ones, they come here to kneel on, to touch, and sometimes to eat, the sacred earth of Chimayó.

And then, they rise, healed and restored, strong again. It has happened over and over again, as the crutches hanging from the walls of the Santuario de Chimayó attest.

They have been coming here for centuries.

Long before the sanctuary was built in 1816, and long before the first Spanish settlers arrived in this secluded valley in the Sangre de Cristo foothills in 1701—long before those relatively contemporary milestones—sick and enfeebled people were drawn to this miraculous place, seeking the curative powers of its magic soil.

The shrine's origins go back to the creation myths of the Tewa Indians. During this period of prehistory, the Twin War Brothers slew the evil giant Ye-itso, causing fire, smoke and boiling water to burst out of the earth in many places. When that great turbulence subsided, the spouting geysers became New Mexico's muddy, steaming hot springs.

Many who live here have experienced the blissful stimulation of these hot springs; people from out-of-state have made periodic journeys here for its medicinal properties as well. The volcanically heated water soaks away tenacious miseries, just as heavy emotional burdens are also washed away in sweat. Visitors to the hot springs experience that exhilarating rush as the pores open, as the lungs fill with the rich vapors rising from the steaming mineral waters. For countless years, the Tewa people enjoyed these same soothing pleasures at the hot springs they called *"Tsimajopokwi"*.

But gradually the pool dried up, leaving only a pit of mud. Finally, it was just dry dirt.

The Tewa word for "pool of water" is *"pok-wi"*. When the water disappeared from Tsimajopokwi, the place came to be called *"Tsimayo";* later still, the place name was altered to "Chimayó".

The Spanish colonizers came to this area after their re-conquest (made necessary by the bloody Pueblo Revolt of 1680) and began settling the Chimayó Valley in about 1701. At first there were only three families, ministered by a priest from San Juan Pueblo. The settlement grew slowly; by 1813 there were still only 19 families. The head of one of these families, Bernardo Abeyta, would become the central figure in the great religious drama which unfolded in the remote but beautiful valley.

Bernardo Abeyta was a pious man, by all accounts, and a member of *Los Hermanos Penitentes del Tercér Orden de Franciscanos* (The Brotherhood of the Penitentes). Surely the United States has never seen a more devout religious order than the New Mexican Penitentes.

Penitentes believed fervently in the rites of penance. They practiced self-flagellation to atone for their sins. They believed it was far better to suffer some in this life than to face an eternity of agony in hell. So strong was their faith that every Good Friday, they performed a literal re-enactment of the biblical Crucifixion, in which a particularly devout follower volunteered to be staked through his hands and feet to an upright cross, in the exact manner of the original event.

Each year in Chimayó, three members of the Penitente Brotherhood were selected to drag enormous wooden crosses up the hill to Calvario. Members of the procession that accompanied the cross bearers lashed themselves with cactus-studded whips; women stuffed their shoes with cactus for the long, painful march.

The *penitente* chosen to portray Christ endured the cruelest... yet most eagerly sought... punishment of all. With a crown of thorns on his head, he was tied, or nailed, to the heavy cross. If he survived this supreme test, he was a revered and politically powerful man thereafter; if he died on the cross, he earned a place in heaven, not only for himself, but for all members of his family.

Clearly, the Penitentes took their religion very seriously.

Their beliefs date back at least as far as the 13th Century, when organized societies of flagellants in Europe flogged themselves to appease the wrathful God who had brought the Black Plague on civilization. In New Mexico, many of the early settlers lived in near-total isolation from the mainstream of Spanish colonial authority, centered in Santa Fe. Since the guidance of priests was only sporadically available to parishioners, they gradually evolved their own rituals and customs. Although severe penances were the dominant aspect of their faith, the Penitentes also organized and maintained a communal society which, in addition to fulfilling spiritual needs, also provided health care, welfare for the needy and a judicial system.

The Penitentes developed special insights about the remote land in which they lived, and so, perhaps, it is not surprising that extraordinary events sometimes occurred in their lives ... events they attributed to their natural environment. The extraordinary event that led to the building of the Santuario de Chimayó is probably the most dramatic and significant of all such episodes.

It occurred during a Holy Week, probably in 1813. Bernardo Abeyta was performing his penances on a hillside above the Rio Santa Cruz. Perhaps the intensity of his self-inflicted pain sharpened his senses, for when he looked up, he saw a bright light shining from the ground not far from the river. He ran to the spot, knelt and began digging with his bare hands toward the source of the light. Within minutes, he had uncovered a large and wondrous cross bearing the carved image of Our Lord of Esquípulas.

Abeyta showed his amazing discovery to Father Sebastián Alvarez, who organized a procession to take the crucifix to the church in Santa Cruz. It was placed in a niche of the main altar, but the next morning, it was gone. The confusion and anxiety that followed was finally relieved when Bernardo Abeyta found the cross back in the same hole. A second procession was formed and the cross was reinstalled in the Santa Cruz church. Once again, it vanished and reappeared in the hole.

After this startling miracle occurred a third time, the villagers realized the crucifix was meant to remain at the place where it was originally discovered, so a tiny chapel was built above the hole.

A short time later, Abeyta became gravely ill. For days, he lay in his bed, sweating feverishly and growing steadily weaker. Finally, he summoned all his remaining strength, rose to his feet, wrapped himself in blankets and stumbled off toward the chapel.

As he neared the holy place, he saw Our Lord of Esquípulas standing there. The figure beckoned to him; Abeyta shed his blankets and staggered forward. Before he reached the apparition, it disappeared. When Abeyta dropped to his knees on the spot where the apparition had stood, he was instantly healed.

That was the first miraculous cure of Chimayó; many more would follow.

One of the more curious aspects of the legendary origins of this healing shrine in north-central New Mexico is that the miracles all centered around Our Lord of Esquípulas. It seems both enigmatic and appropriate that the cross Abeyta found bore the crucified image of *Nuestro Señor de Esquípulas*—the Black Christ of Guatemala.

The Guatemalan town of Esquípulas is more than 2,000 miles from the village of Chimayó. In 1813, neither town was likely to have been aware of the other's existence, though it is possible the residents of Chimayó may have heard rumors of the Guatemalan cult of *El Cristo Negro*.

The legend of the Black Christ and the miraculous cures that take place in Esquípulas' massive baroque church pre-date the Chimayó cures by nearly 300 years. During the Spanish conquest of Central America, the Mayan Indians in southeastern Guatemala surrendered to the invaders and agreed to accept the Catholic faith. However, they had endured so much of the Spaniards' cruelty that they were deeply suspicious of the symbol of a white Christ.

The Catholic church commissioned a famed woodcarver, Quirio Catano, to carve a life-size *cristo* out of brown wood, rightly surmising that the Indians would find this image more acceptable since its natural color was closer to their own skin color. The crucifix bearing the brown *cristo* was housed in a small chapel built on the site of a Mayan shrine, close to several sulphurous hot springs. Over the years, smoke from incense burned at the altar turned this carving a smoky black color.

The name of the leader of his group of Indians was pronounced *Es-KIP-ur-ha*, so the village that grew up around the shrine became known as Esquípulas.

Soon, miraculous cures began to take place in the chapel. Pilgrims started coming from far and wide. When the Archbishop of Guatemala, Pedro Pardo de Figueroa, was cured of a contagious disease during his visit to the shrine in 1758, he ordered a sanctuary built on the site. During the next two centuries, thousands more people were cured of a variety of minor and major ailments.

Though a strong faith is considered a necessary factor in any miraculous healing, the soil of the Santuario de Esquípulas seemed to be of equal importance. The people of Esquípulas began manufacturing tiny, white clay tablets from the earth at their holy site. They embossed these *benditos* with pictures of *El Cristo Negro*, and the tablets were blessed by local priests. Pilgrims could buy the pills and take them on the spot, dissolve the tablets in water to drink the clay earth, or take the medicine home to their relatives.

The clay from which the tablets are made is a finely-grained kaolin, often used in the manufacture of ceramics. Its principal ingredient is hydrous aluminum silicate, along with traces of iron oxide, magnesia, sodium, potassium and calcium. Kaolin has long been used as a treatment for diarrhea, but the chemical composition of the *benditos* of Esquípulas cannot account for the reported cures of paralysis, rheumatism and the alleviation of pain in childbirth.

The people who kneel at the shrines in Esquípulas and in Chimayó have much in common, even though they are geographically and culturally far apart.

Both Guatemala and Chimayó were first settled by Indian people who were later subjugated by Spanish conquerors and forced to integrate their ancient religious beliefs into the alien and awesome fabric of European Catholicism. And, in both places, people hung a special image of Christ above the altar in the sanctuaries: a smoke-blackened *Cristo Negro* in Esquípulas, and a pale gold *Cristo* in Chimayó.

In both places, people eat the earth and unexplainable miraculous healings take place.

Clay-eating, or geophagy, has been a widespread custom throughout history and has been practiced by both the Mayans and the Indians of the American Southwest. However, the village of Chimayó is the only place in the Southwest where pilgrimages of both Indians and Hispanics lead to a Catholic shrine to partake of the *tierra bendita,* the blessed earth.

After word of Bernardo Abeyta's miraculous recovery spread among the settlers in 1813, many other people traveled to the same spot, knelt and were also cured of their medical problems. Abeyta was so impressed that he wrote to Padre Alvarez requesting permission to build a *santuario* to "honor and venerate with worthy worship, our Lord and Redeemer, in his Advocation of Esquípulas". Alvarez presented the request to the Vicar General of the Diocese, who forwarded it to the Archbishop in Durango, Mexico, who granted permission in April 1815 to build a church at the Chimayó site.

The Santuario de Chimayó was completed the following year. It is indeed an impressive structure. Built by communal labor, it is 90 feet long, 30 feet wide and its walls are over three feet thick. *El Posito,* the hole or sacred well from which the miraculous earth is obtained, is housed in a special candle-lit room behind the sacristy. On the wall of the sacristy itself, dozens of crutches and canes hang in clusters, left there by prilgrims who experienced cures.

Surely any small village would be proud to have such a fine church, with such an incredible reputation. Surprisingly enough, Chimayó has not just one miraculous church, but two.

Sometime between 1850 and 1860, an additional miracle is said to have occurred near Chimayó—a miracle that led to the building of a private chapel dedicated to the *Santo Niño.*

One day, a villager named Severiano Medina was driving his cattle to his fields, accompanied by his young daughter. Suddenly, the little girl heard a church bell ringing beneath the ground. She called to her father, and when he, too, heard the sound, they began to dig. Soon he unearthed a bell, and upon digging deeper, discovered a wooden statue of the *Santo Niño de Atocha.*

Many people came to see this wonderous statue, and those who were ill became well when they knelt before it. A private chapel to house the *Santo Niño* was established just west of the Santuario de Chimayó. Over the years, the two churches rivaled each other for the number of cures they produced.

Perhaps the most famous person to be healed by the *Santo Niño* was María Martinez, the renown potter of San Ildefonso Pueblo. When she was just a child, she became seriously ill. Her mother made a vow to the Holy Child that if their daughter recovered, she would make a pilgrimage to the statue's shrine. María, too, prayed fervently. The healing was granted, the vow was kept, and María Martinez went on to become one of New Mexico's most revered artisans.

The *Santo Niño's* healing powers are not exclusively reserved for those who visit the shrine. It is widely believed that the tiny, doll-like figure departs the chapel at night and travels around the countryside, secretly listening to the people's evening prayer and granting their earnest requests. As a result of the *Santo Niño's* nocturnal wanderings, his little shoes are scuffed and worn out.

New Mexico's Penitente country is laden with an uncommon intensity of faith, pain and hope. Undercurrents of religious fervor run so deep that the miracles of Chimayó should hardly seem surprising.

HOW TO GET TO THE BLESSED EARTH OF CHIMAYO

Chimayó can easily be reached by driving the picturesque curves of State Highway 76, east of Española. Both the Santuario de Chimayó and the Santo Niño Chapel are centrally located within the village, surrounded by unique stores where one can purchase both holy medallions and superb tamales.

BIBLIOGRAPHY

THE BLESSED EARTH OF CHIMAYO
Chapter Five

Bullock, Alice. **Living Legends of the Santa Fe Country.** Denver, Colo. Green Mountain Press. 1970.

Boyd E. "Señor Santiago de Chimayó", *El Palacio,* March 1956.

Cardona-Hine, Alvaro. "The Whip and the Cross", *Mankind,* June, 1974.

de Borhegyi, Stephen. **El Santuario de Chimayó.** Milwaukee, Wis. Milwaukee Public Museum. 1961.

de Borhegyi, Stephen. "The Cult of Our Lord of Esquípulas", *El Palacio,* December, 1954.

de Borhegyi, Stephen. "Miraculous Shrines", *El Palacio,* March 1953.

Prince, L. Bradford. **Spanish Mission Churches of New Mexico.** Cedar Rapids, Iowa. The Torch Press. 1915.

6
MIRACLES OF OLD SANTA FE

Legends hover, like piñón smoke on a winter's night, in the ancient city of Santa Fe. Little wonder that Santa Fe was chosen as the state capital of the Land of Enchantment.

Nor is it surprising that most of its mysteries and miracles have occurred in its grand old churches. How could it be that so many superb and enduring cathedrals and chapels would arise in an isolated little town in a neglected part of the American frontier? The magnificence of the native-stone towers of the Cathedral of St. Francis, the thick adobe walls of Our Lady of Guadalupe and the massive bulk of El Cristo Rey would be impressive enough if they were the only ones. But there are many others.

The Church of San Miguél is the oldest in the United States. Built in 1610, a full decade before the Mayflower set sail, San Miguél is one of the most frequently visited chapels in New Mexico. Its location on the corner of Old Santa Fe Trail and De Vargas Street, across from the oldest European home in the United

States, makes it easily accessible to tourists. The chapel houses many splendid antiques, but its finest attraction is the great Andalusian bell which now hangs in San Miguél's souvenir room.

The bell weighs 780 pounds, is four inches thick, and is said to yield the sweetest-toned chime in America. It is also the oldest. Cast in 1356, thousands of miles from New Mexico, the San Miguél bell played a significant role in the history of Spain.

In the mid-1300s, the Catholics of Spain were fighting the Islamic Moors for control of Europe's Iberian Peninsula. In battle after battle, the Catholics were being overwhelmed by the inspired ferocity of the "infidels". Finally, the Spaniards vowed a bell to St. Joseph for his assistance in bringing them victory. The people brought their gold, silver and jewelry to add to other metals in a huge melting pot. When the bell was cast, its inscription read *"San José, ruega por nosotros"* . . . "St. Joseph, pray for us."

Apparently the offering helped, for the tide of the battles turned, giving victory to the Catholics. Centuries later, the religious historian Reverend W.J. Howlett wrote that the bell rang with "the richness of gold and the sweetness of sacrifice. It sounded the defeat of Moslemism in Spain, and then came to ring in the birth of Christianity in Mexico, and with the Padres it found its way up the Rio Grande to rest and ring out its sweet notes over the City of the Holy Faith."

It was the already centuries-old bell dedicated to St. Joseph during the Spanish *Reconquista* that wound up in one of the most remote outposts of far-flung Spanish colonial empire in the 1600s. The bell seems to have arrived in Santa Fe with its powers intact, for there is a second legend associated with it which—though lacking the enormous geo-political significance of the first—is still very poignant.

As the legend is told, an old blind man used to pray each day at noon in the San Miguél Chapel where the historic bell was hung. He did not pray to St. Joseph, however, but to St. Cecilia, patron saint of music. As he prayed, the great bell would begin to ring, though no human hands pulled the bell rope. And for as long as the bell tolled, the old man's blindness left him.

He could accurately describe the altar before him, and the carved *reredos* behind it; he could count the great vigas in the ceiling, and could identify the colors in the chapel's magnificent paintings. Then, when the bell stopped ringing, his world again grew dark and he was blind once more.

The priests tried to bring back his sight by tolling the bell themselves, but only when the ancient bell rang of its own accord could the blind man see.

The name of the blind man, and the date of this recurring miracle, are unknown, but it must have been prior to 1872. In that year, the bell fell from its 50-foot tower during a violent storm. Since that time, it has been suspended on a sturdy wooden frame on the ground floor, and has not rung by itself since the anonymous blind man died.

Another of Santa Fe's religious artifacts is alleged to have been responsible for at least two miracles. The exquisite little statue of the Virgin Mary, known as *"La Conquistadora"*, Our Lady of the Conquest, also traveled incredible distances, just as the Andalusian bell, before reaching its permanent home in Santa Fe.

The exact age of this lovely willow-wood carving is unknown, and the date of its journey from the Old World to the New is unrecorded. We do know that the statue began its first journey to New Mexico in 1625, when a Franciscan monk, Fray Alonso de Benavides, arranged to have it sent by oxcart from Mexico City to the heart of New Spain—the village of Santa Fe.

At that time, the statue was called "Our Lady of the Conception", and it stood in a small shrine at the Santa Fe parish church for the next 55 years. That era was not one in which Santa Feans could take much pride. Corruption in government and brutal, shameless exploitation of the enslaved Pueblo Indians by the local aristocracy largely characterized those times. Even some of the friars were abusive and contemptuous of their Indian converts; Christianity was getting a very bad reputation in New Mexico. The devout were sure it was only a matter of time before a heavy price would have to be paid for the un-Christian behavior of the sinful, avaricious minority.

The warning of that impending calamity came on a night in 1674.

Late that evening, a ten-year-old girl awoke from a feverish sleep in her bed in Santa Fe. The child had been very ill for days, and had prayed ardently to the Holy Virgin for a cure. Suddenly, the Virgin appeared before the trembling girl, saying, "Daughter, rise up." The little girl stood and her illness was instantly gone.

Then the apparition told her the Empire of New Spain was soon to be destroyed for its lack of reverence. The Virgin told the girl that her miraculous cure was meant to be proof that the Virgin had, indeed, spoken to her and that she should pass her message on to the other settlers.

When the child told of the Virgin's appearance, she spoke so convincingly that most people took the message quite seriously; many began to mend their wicked ways. Others felt that since the destruction was inevitable anyway, repentance would be meaningless, so they continued to live as they had previously. Still others scoffed. Why should anyone believe the words of a mere child?

The prophecy was fulfilled on August 10, 1680.

On that fateful day, the Pueblo Indians rose up as a united people and—for the first and only time in the history of our nation—drove the European invaders completely out of the country. They struck, almost simultaneously, at every Spanish settlement in New Spain, either killing the inhabitants or forcing them to flee. They attacked Santa Fe on August 15.

The Santa Feans barricaded themselves in the Palace of the Governors as the Indians surrounded the town. The Pueblo warriors set fire to the abandoned Spanish houses and churches and, as the town burned, they laid seige to the adobe-walled palace. As always, the Indians paid a terrible price for their audacity. Their arrows and warclubs were no match for the muskets and steel swords of the armor-clad Spanish horsemen who rode out of the gates and slashed their way into the attacking Indians. By the end of the first day, scores of Indians were dead, and only five Spaniards had been killed. Still, many Spanish soldiers had been wounded and their fighting capacity was greatly weakened. The Indians, in spite of their losses, grew stronger as more warriors arrived from the northern pueblos to take the place of those who had fallen.

The siege lasted nine days; when the Indians diverted the ditch that supplied the palace's water, the Spanish knew they were defeated. They formed a caravan and, with a military escort of battered soldiers, made a long, bedraggled retreat to El Paso del Norte.

Just before the attack on Santa Fe began, a woman named Josefa Lopez Sambrano de Grijalva had the presence of mind to remove Our Lady of the Conception from its shrine and took the holy statue into the temporary shelter of the Palace of the Governors. Had she not done so, this famous image of the Virgin Mary would have been consumed in the fire that destroyed the parish church. And had Josefa not carried this special statue in her arms all the way to El Paso, the miracles of the Spaniards' later reconquest might not have occurred.

For the next 12 years, the statue and the displaced people of New Spain lived in exile near the banks of the Rio del Norte, dreaming of their return one day to Santa Fe. In 1692, the Spanish government at last sent a man who, with the help of the Virgin, would be able to fulfill these people's dreams.

His name was Don Diego de Vargas, and to say that he changed the history of New Mexico more than any other man is something of an understatement. Don

Diego was a *conquistador* . . . a conqueror for the Spanish Crown. But he was also a persuasive negotiator, a man who could not only lead an army, but could talk his enemies out of fighting. He was a pious man who believed the reconversion of the Indians was the highest priority of his personal *Reconquista*.

In 1692, Don Diego led his small but heavily-armed expedition up the Rio Grande Valley and rode boldly into Santa Fe. Aware of his return, Indian forces had assembled in the plaza. Dismounting, Don Diego approached and embraced each Indian leader. It was time, he said, for the Indian and the Spanish to live in peace, time for forgiveness and a restoration of the Holy Faith. To emphasize the fact that he would not take "no" for an answer, he also aimed a cannon at them.

The Indians debated for several hours. After they were assured they would never again be whipped or forced to labor against their will, they raised a large cross in the plaza. The Reconquest of Santa Fe was accomplished without bloodshed.

And so it went at each of the pueblos: Don Diego de Vargas led his well-armed troops to each Indian settlement, accepted their submission, and then the accompanying friars absolved the Indians of their sins. By December, Don Diego was back in El Paso del Norte, ready to organize and escort the displaced colonists back to what remained of their former homes.

On October 4, 1693, the caravan headed north, consisting of 70 families, 100 soldiers, 18 friars, dozens of servants and thousands of cattle, horses and mules. With them came Our Lady of the Conception in an altar cart. It was an arduous journey; 30 women and children died crossing the vast wastelands of southern New Spain. It was winter by the time the settlers reached the base of La Bajada Hill, just south of Santa Fe.

The long escarpment of La Bajada had always been a barrier to travelers. Although it has since been conquered by a freeway, it was a formidable obstacle in Don Diego's time. He faced a near-superhuman task in getting his wagon train to the crest that winter. The old, pre-rebellion road had completely washed away in the 13 years of disuse. Though the people in the caravan labored along side the mules and oxen to pull the wagons and cargo up the hill, they were still far below the summit after two days of backbreaking toil. One vehicle in particular proved especially stubborn. No amount of effort could move the altar cart up La Bajada.

Though the oxen strained, the cart's wheels would not turn. Many sturdy men put their shoulders to the cart, pushing it and even trying to lift it, but the wheels seemed to have sprouted roots among the rocks.

Don Diego knew this was a sign from the sacred representation of the Virgin Mary inside the cart. He knelt beside the immovable wheels and made a vow: if he were allowed to take his caravan on to Santa Fe, he would build a chapel there with a special shrine for Our Lady of the Conception. Once the vow was made, the altar cart rolled easily and soon all the people, wagons and animals reached the top of La Bajada.

In Santa Fe, they found the situation changed drastically during the past year. The Indians were having second thoughts about having capitulated so easily. They had built a wall around the plaza and were ready to defend it. Don Diego spoke to them, promised them a new pueblo at Santa Clara and gave them one week to vacate the plaza. He camped his weary column near the spot where Santa Fe's National Cemetery is now located.

The weather was bitterly cold and snow covered the ground. Don Diego de Vargas waited two weeks for the Indians to leave the plaza, but the barricaded walls only grew higher as the Indians prepared for a fight. After 21 Spaniards died of exposure in their miserable camp, Don Diego again knelt beside the altar cart and reaffirmed his vow. If Our Lady of the Conception would grant him a victory, he would build the promised chapel on exactly the spot where the cart now rested. In the morning, he unleashed his soldiers against the Indian battlements.

The fight lasted all day, but by nightfall, the walls still had not been breached. Don Diego withdrew his forces to the campsite. He asked everyone to pray with him. Soldiers, colonists, friars and servants all dropped to their knees in the snow to pray for help from the tiny statue. Arising, Don Diego led his soldiers silently off into the night.

Under cover of darkness, his men swarmed over the walls and caught the Indian defenders by surprise. In the carnage that followed, the Indians were completely defeated, survivors fleeing into the cold, dark mountains. Santa Fe once again was a Spanish possession.

As the rebuilding of the town got under way, Don Diego de Vargas wrote to the Viceroy of New Spain, expressing his wish to build "a church and holy temple, setting up in it before all else the patroness of the said kingdom and villa, who is the one that was saved from the fury of the savages, her title being Our Lady of the Conquest."

Don Diego would never see the chapel built; he never fulfilled his vow to the Virgin. During the turbulent decade that followed his reconquest, he found himself engaged in new battles which could not be won with swords. Political rivals came from Mexico City, deposed him as governor and jailed him for years on charges of malfeasance in office. By the time he cleared his name, he was in poor health. He died April 8, 1704.

Our Lady of the Conception, now renamed Our Lady of the Conquest and called *"La Conquistadora"* for short, resided in a temporary parish church behind the rebuilt Palace of the Governors. The colonists did their best to honor the statue while they waited until a new chapel could be built. Each year, *La Conquista-*

dora was carried to the site of the encampment, placed in a shrine of pine boughs and, for nine days, masses were chanted. At last, in 1806, a wealthy Santa Fean, Antonio José Ortiz, built Rosario Chapel on the site.

By that time, the little statue had found a home in St. Francis Cathedral, at Santa Fe's Francisco Street and Cathedral Place. But the tradition of the novena for *La Conquistadora* continued, with the statue carried in procession each year to Rosario Chapel.

The miracles of Old Santa Fe are mostly those presented in history books or legends from a far-off time. But there is one miracle of Old Santa Fe that can still be seen and experienced to this day: we can stand beside it, touch it and marvel, even though this particular miracle occurred more than a hundred years ago.

On Old Santa Fe Trail, just past San Miguél Chapel, stands a small, elegant Gothic chapel. At first glance, it looks a little out of place in Santa Fe. Its pointed arches and medieval columns seem better suited to the countryside of France. And, in fact, it was copied after Sainte Chapelle in Paris.

Santa Fe's Loretto Chapel was the realization of Archbishop John B. Lamy's most cherished dream. Though he commissioned construction of many of Santa Fe's early religious and educational buildings, his greatest ambition was to erect a special chapel, one that would equal the finest chapels of Europe.

Work on Loretto Chapel began in 1873, but proceeded slowly as a variety of problems developed. The original architect, Antoine Mouly, lost his eyesight and had to abandon the project. His son, Projectus Mouly, was hired to continue the design work. But, as it turned out, the younger Mouly's eyesight may have been a bit too sharp. He is said to have spent more time eyeing the local ladies than attending to his architectural drawings.

Projectus began paying visits to the wife of the nephew of Archbishop Lamy while the nephew was not at home. When the cuckold husband learned of these trysts, he ordered Mouly, under threat of death, never to set foot in his home again. The wife responded by moving into Mouly's room at the Exchange Hotel. Next day, the brief little romance ended abruptly as Projectus Mouly walked out of the room and found Lamy's nephew waiting for him in the hallway, pistol in hand.

So it was that the people of Santa Fe were left with a dead architect and an unfinished set of construction plans. But the plans ... incomplete as they were ... looked very good, so ground was broken and the chapel began to rise. It was almost completed before anyone noticed that there was a major flaw in the otherwise sublime design. Mouly, at the time of his demise, had not yet figured out a way to include a stairway to the choirloft. And now it was too late to do anything about it.

A conventional staircase inside the church would be an awkward intrusion into the nave and would displace many pews. Yet a stairway built onto an outside wall would spoil the symmetrical balance of the Parisian-styled chapel. There appeared to be no solution to the problem. The distraught Sisters of Loretto Academy took the matter into their own hands. They made a novena to St. Joseph, patron saint of carpenters. On the ninth morning of their special prayers, the Mother Superior, Magdalen Hayden, received a strange visitor. To the doors of the convent came a white-haired, bearded old man, leading a burro. He had come to build the stairway, he said. Taken aback, Mother Magdalen could only nod her approval.

There must have been something about the old man himself that impressed the Mother Superior, for the strange carpenter's tools were not at all impressive. He was equipped only with a T-square, a saw and a hammer; he asked only for two big tubs, filled with water.

The enigmatic craftsman worked alone, in complete privacy. Whenever the sisters entered to pray, he

THE MIRACULOUS STAIRCASE. The unsupported spiral staircase in Santa Fe's Loretto Chapel mystifies those who behold it.

Photo by LaDonna Kutz

quietly left. They noticed pieces of wood soaking in the tubs, though the carpenter had purchased no wood locally.

At last, the stairway was finished. Those that beheld it could scarcely believe their eyes. Before them stood a spiral staircase like none they had ever seen. It rose from the floor to the loft in two complete 360-degree swirls. Its perfect curves were spliced in seven places on the inside and nine on the outside. Wooden pegs, rather than nails, had been used throughout. But most miraculously of all, the staircase had no central support. There was nothing holding it up.

It had no railing and looked so fragile that adults were afraid to climb it. So the first ascent was made by young girls from the Loretto Academy. They climbed it cautiously and were so frightened when they reached the top that they came back down on hands and knees.

The sisters' prayers had been answered; this incredible architectural afterthought was now the most fantastic feature of the chapel. The nuns set about preparing a festive meal to honor the stairway's creator, but when they sent for the old carpenter, he could not be found. His work finished, he disappeared without receiving either pay or recognition.

The Miraculous Staircase became a major visitor attraction, as much for local Santa Feans as tourists. Men from the local lumberyard were particularly perplexed; the wood used for the spiral staircase was not indigenous to New Mexico.

Five years later, a dark-wood railing was added to the stairway and its splendor was completed. But the mystery of its construction remained.

In 1965, a consulting engineer, Carl R. Albach, felt he might have discovered part of the reason that the unsupported staircase doesn't collapse. He had been hired to redesign the chapel's main electrical service and meter loop. In the course of his work, Albach climbed the stairs several times. Each time he went up or down, he was aware of a small amount of vertical movement, as if the two 360-degree turns were taken out of a large, coiled spring. He discussed this slight buoyancy with the Mother Superior, who said she, too, had noticed a certain amount of springiness. Perhaps the Miraculous Staircase stands the way a coiled spring will stand if it is perfectly balanced.

The identity of the mysterious carpenter has never been learned, but the Sisters of Loretto Academy were sure they knew who he was. They made that very clear when they named this work of art "St. Joseph's Stairway".

HOW TO GET TO MIRACLES OF OLD SANTA FE

A tour of Santa Fe's miraculous churches can begin at San Miguél Chapel on the corner of old Santa Fe Trail and de Vargas Street. A short walk north on Old Santa Fe Trail brings you to Loretto Chapel. St. Francis is just east of La Fonda, on Cathedral Place. Rosario Chapel is also close by. From St. Francis Cathedral, follow San Francisco Street west to Guadalupe Street, which leads north to Rosario Chapel, a half-mile away.

BIBLIOGRAPHY

MIRACLES OF OLD SANTA FE
Chapter Six

Alback, Carl R. "Miracle or Wonder of Construction?" *Consulting Engineer.* December 1965.

Bullock, Alice. **Living Legends of the Santa Fe Country.** Denver, Colo. Green Mountain Press. 1970.

Capper's Weekly. "Mysterious Old Man Built Miracle Staircase in Santa Fe". Topeka, Kan. Stauffer Publications. May, 1972.

Chavez, Fray Angélico. **La Conquistadora.** Santa Fe, N.M. Historical Society of New Mexico. 1948.

Chavez, Fray Angélico. "Our Lady of the Conquest", *El Palacio.* Spring, 1985.

Horgan, Paul. **Great River, Vol. I.** New York. Holt, Rinehart and Winston. 1954.

Prince L. Bradford. **Spanish Mission Churches of New Mexico.** Cedar Rapids, Iowa. The Torch Press. 1915.

Segale, Sister Blandina. **At the End of the Santa Fe Trail.** Milwaukee, Wis. Bruce Publishing Company. 1948.

7
AMBUSHES IN DOG CANYON

In the sweltering heat of an August afternoon in 1878, U.S. Cavalry Captain Carroll Henry halted his small troop at the mouth of a narrow canyon on the edge of the Sacramento Mountains. His men slumped wearily on their horses; their sweat-stained uniforms were caked with dust from the long ride across the Tularosa Basin. Several of the troopers suffered from the effects of prolonged thirst.

Earlier, Captain Henry had shared his last canteen . . . one tepid swallow per man. Now, he turned in his saddle to stare back over the wasteland his column had just crossed. The blazing irradiance of White Sands seemed to float near the horizon. Somewhere among the shimmering desert heat waves, Henry knew the pack mules of the supply train were following his tracks. He realized now the mules could not reach his troop before dark.

Turning his attention the the canyon ahead, he remained convinced the trail of the Indians he sought led there unmistakably. He was sure, though not especially happy, that the Indians had disappeared into the canyon's narrow confines. With a wave of his arm, Captain Henry ordered his troops forward; the exhausted column stumbled on.

In the canyon, not a breath of air was stirring; high walls and bluffs rose to stifle all breezes from the outside. Captain Henry would later write that it was like riding through a furnace, that never before had he felt the heat so intensely. Deeper in the ravine, the passage narrowed still more. Great ocher-colored walls towered above the trail; the soldiers nervously eyed a drop of several hundred feet just to the left of their horses' hooves.

A growing sense of apprehension passed through the ranks. The trail was now so narrow that the men found themselves strung out in single file. Though the Indians' tracks led clearly, almost inexorably onward, there was not a sign of movement nor a sound to break the stillness. Captain Henry hesitated briefly, listened intently, then pushed on.

Suddenly there was a burst of gunfire. Men toppled from their mounts and horses fell screaming down the slopes. Simultaneously, from the heights above came a thunder-like rumble. For one puzzled moment, the cavalrymen froze. Then came the realization that tons of boulders were bounding down from the cliffs to crash onto the line of horsemen. Panic seized men and beasts alike; the soldiers jerked frantically at the reins as their terrified, rearing mounts pitched over the side.

A second volley ripped through the churning figures and echoed off the cliffs. Captain Henry's unfortunate troopers fired back blindly. In desperation, they fought their way back down the treacherous trail and out of the gorge . . . survivors of another ambush in Dog Canyon.

Probably no other single locale in the West has been the setting for more violence than New Mexico's

Dog Canyon. Between 1859 and 1881, at least three major engagements and several smaller skirmishes were fought in this spectacular ravine.

Later, during the bitter range wars of the 1880s, the canyon again became a battleground. Death, it seemed, was as much a part of Dog Canyon as were its cliffs and eerie shadows. It is not surprising that all of the battles were ambushes, for nowhere in the Southwest can one find a place better suited to that deadly tactic.

Cañón del Perro, Canyon of the Dog, lies eleven miles south of Alamogordo. Here, on the geologic line that separates 500 square miles of desert from the cool, piney mountains beyond, the rugged Sacramento Escarpment abruptly rises, creased and cut by deep canyons. Few of the canyons have water; *Cañón del Perro* does. It also has walls 2,000 feet high and it ends in a box. At the vertical headwall, there is only one way up and out of the canyon ... a precarious passage on the Eyebrow Trail. Dog Canyon is a natural trap.

Ordinarily, traps are something to be avoided, yet for a period of nearly 50 years, Dog Canyon drew scores of people into its lonely depths and, time after time, they were ambushed. The number of fatalities in this small, middle-of-nowhere canyon are unrecorded, but the death toll is well over 100.

The first recorded ambush there took place in February 1859. On February 8, 32 men under the command of Lieutenant H.M. Lazelle set out from Fort Bliss, Texas, to track down a band of Apaches reported to have stolen a herd of cattle and some mules three days earlier. Lazelle and his men covered 165 miles in seven days. They found no water along their route. During the sixth day, "the soldiers had a swallow of water, the horses none." At noon on the seventh day, the trail led into Dog Canyon.

The troopers rode unopposed for two and a half miles up the gorge. Then they met a group of 30 warriors, painted and armed, but carrying a white flag of truce. The Apaches asked the purpose of the white men's mission. Told they were accused of rustling livestock, the warriors claimed to be innocent. Some "bad men" had done it, they said, adding that they themselves had chased the bad men away and recovered the cattle.

Unconvinced, Lieutenant Lazelle ignored the white flag and launched an attack. Immediately he and his men were caught in a withering barrage of rifle fire from above. Beleaguered from the the side and in front, Lazelle had no choice but to retreat. Gathering up as many of his wounded as possible, he ran the gauntlet out of the canyon, losing several more men along the way.

Not all of Dog Canyon's battles were won by Indians. In 1863, General James H. Carleton ordered Colonel Christopher "Kit" Carson to commence a campaign against the Apaches. In a sweeping pincer movement, Carson sent Major William McCleave's company south from Fort Stanton while Captains Roberts and McKee brought their troops up from El Paso. They planned to meet at Dog Canyon and combine forces for an attack on the Apache *rancherías* in the Sacramento Mountains.

McCleave reached the canyon first. On March 27, he camped his men and horses before sending scouts into the notorious ravine. The scouts were back quickly with news of a nearby Mescalero camp, still blissfully unaware of the soldiers' presence.

Major McCleave wasted no time to press his advantage. The element of surprise was on the side of the cavalry this time, and they slipped quietly into the canyon. Their sudden attack swept through the wicki-ups in a rout that produced only one casualty among the cavalrymen while the Mescaleros lost 25 men as they scrambled up the slopes.

Once they reached higher ground, the Apaches rallied and staged a counter-attack. In the reprisal, Lieu-

DOG CANYON. A hiker walks on the Eyebrow Trail beneath the cliffs that have echoed time and time again with murderous gunfire.

Photo by Jack Kutz

tenant French and one enlisted man were wounded. But McCleave's men were flushed with the fighting spirit. They charged straight up the rugged slopes, fighting boulder to boulder, killing three more Indians and scattering the rest.

A few days later, the entire Apache band appeared at Fort Stanton to surrender to Colonel Carson.

Even so, troubles between the white man and the Apache were far from resolved. When reservation life proved intolerable, the Indians once again took to the warpath. Throughout the bloody years that followed, Dog Canyon continued to play an important role. One by one, the Apache bands met defeat. In 1881, Nana's band became the last hostile Apaches to camp in Dog Canyon. Finally the aging warrior fled to Mexico; the steep canyon, so ready-made for blood-letting, at last stood empty and peaceful.

The respite was of short duration. In 1884, a man of an entirely different sort entered Dog Canyon and its history: François Jean Rochas. No one will ever know what attracted the Frenchman to the canyon, nor why he left family and friends behind in France to spend the rest of his life scratching out a subsistence living, alone in the desolate desert gorge. To the people of the Tularosa Basin, he was simply Frenchy, the hermit of Dog Canyon.

Frenchy was eccentric, no denying that, but he was also a man of great determination and rare courage. His first battle in Dog Canyon was a fight against the land. Using the stones around him, he built a cabin and walls to define and contain his domain. He planted and hand-watered a garden and small orchard in Dog Canyon; he even managed to graze a few cattle as well. In his own hard-scramble way, Frenchy made the desert bloom.

His next battle involved a thief with a rifle.

One morning, while Frenchy worked in his garden, a horse thief named Morrison came into the canyon. Morrison apparently knew about the hermit, and that the old recluse had a couple of pretty good horses and a small herd of cattle. For Morrison, it was a target too tempting to resist.

The outlaw crept down through the rocks, took careful aim and opened fire on the old man in his garden. The first shot knocked Frenchy to the ground and the second shattered his arm when he tried to get to his feet. Still, the old man dragged himself back to his stone cabin.

Throughout the long day, Morrison sat in the shade, waiting for Frenchy to bleed to death. After dark, he pushed the cabin door open to inspect his murderous work. Frenchy's pistol roared. The tough little Frenchman was still very much alive; Morrison ran off through the night, howling in pain. Though there is no report of his ever being captured, Morrison never bothered the hermit again.

After recovering, Frenchy continued to live alone, jealously guarding his land. The broken down walls of his cabin stand in the canyon to this day as mute testimony to Frenchy's spirit.

Beyond the canyon, on the desert's edge, another home once stood, far grander than Frenchy's humble cabin. It boasted long, shady porches, elegant doors and big rooms spread out under an expensive tin roof. The land around it was called the Dog Canyon Ranch, and the man who built it was destined to leave his mark on the land and the history books.

His name was Oliver Lee.

It was a name that came to be feared, hated and respected—a name shrouded in terrible secrets. Oliver Lee gained a reputation so fearful that it has been said children broke into tears when they saw him on the street.

He was an insatiably ambitious man. No one stood in his way for very long. In 1888, he clashed with another powerful rancher, John Good, over the proper ownership of several calves. What both range barons really wanted was total control of the harsh rangelands outside Dog Canyon. All it took to set off a bloody range war was a small herd of unbranded strays.

Oliver Lee sent one of his best cowboys, a young man named George McDonald, up into Dog Canyon to round up the disputed calves. At the upper spring, McDonald laid down to rest a moment, apparently falling asleep. His bullet-riddled body was found there a few days later. It was obvious that Lee's cowhand never knew what hit him: he was stretched out comfortably with his feet crossed, his shattered head still pillowed on a blood-stained rock.

An old photograph exists of George McDonald. He is standing against a painted backdrop in a photographer's studio, wearing two cartridge belts and posing as if he might be ready to go for his gun. Yet his youthful bravado did him no good when he made the fatal mistake of dozing off in Dog Canyon.

McDonald's murder remains a mystery, but it did not go unavenged. To Oliver Lee, the killing meant rival John Good had thrown down the gauntlet. Lee's range hands retaliated and John Good's son, Walter, turned up dead, his body dumped on the rippled dunes of White Sands. Following the funeral, Lee and his gunmen opened fire on the mourners; the range war was on in earnest.

Nightriders prowled the ranches; houses were burned. Oliver Lee was arrested, tried and acquitted . . . no one would testify against him.

John Good knew he was beaten. Within a year, he sold out and moved away. Lee's dream of an empire around Dog Canyon had come true. Now only one man still held out against him: the cranky old Frenchman waiting out his days alone in the little stone cabin.

Three days after Christmas in 1894, a cowboy named Dan Fitchett rode out to pay Frenchy a visit. Fitchett knew the hermit was a contrary old duffer, but, like many other folks in Otero County, he sort of liked the old fellow anyway. As Fitchett rode up, he noticed the cabin door was open. Inside, he found the hermit's body sprawled on the floor.

Someone had kicked open the door and shot Frenchy Rochas point-blank as he was writing his Christmas letters. The letters scattered on the floor beside the overturned table were all to his relatives overseas. Frenchy had died thinking of France.

Some folks swore ... though not in court ... that it was Oliver Lee who kicked open Frenchy's door that night. Lee's power continued to grow. His name was linked to more mysteries, such as the disappearance of Albert Jennings Fountain, and the death of Pat Garrett. Through all the whispered accusations, Lee continued his climb to power, eventually becoming a New Mexico state senator. He died of old age in 1941.

It seems fitting that the last known ambush in Dog Canyon was openly perpetrated by Oliver Lee.

In 1899, an Otero County school teacher, J.C. Smith, challenged Lee's claim to Frenchy Rochas' water rights. Smith held the land for several years after the hermit's death. In 1907, the teacher decided to fence off Dog Canyon. For Oliver Lee, that was the last straw. Lee and his men rode out to Dog Canyon, caught the fencing party off-guard and opened fire. A lively shoot-out resulted, ending in Smith's receiving a bullet wound in his hip pocket.

Lee dismissed the whole episode later by declaring, "If I'd wanted him dead, I'd have aimed a little higher."

Oliver Lee eventually moved to town and ran his operations from a big house in Alamogordo. Dog Canyon finally returned to what it had been before the bloody intrusions of mankind—a quiet sanctuary. Today it is protected as a state park, ironically named after Oliver Lee. The upper portion of the canyon is classified as an historic site by the U.S. Forest Service. Its modest little stream still polishes the rocky floor and the steep walls still soak in the burning sun.

Dog Canyon itself hasn't changed much over the years. The only real difference is that it's a whole lot safer there nowadays.

HOW TO GET TO DOG CANYON

Oliver Lee State Park is located four miles east of Valmont, off Highway 54, 11 miles south of Alamogordo. The ruins of Frenchy's cabin are just a hundred yards west of the park visitor's center. The Eyebrow Trail also begins at the center.

The trail traverses the canyon's north-facing slope for 2.4 miles until it reaches a tumbled down stone line cabin. From the cabin, the trail turns north and narrows to a single-file path, etched across a steep slope beneath near vertical cliffs. It was along this .7-mile stretch that Captain Henry's troops were ambushed in 1878.

BIBLIOGRAPHY

AMBUSHES IN DOG CANYON
Chapter Seven

Hutchinson, William Henry. **Another Verdict for Oliver Lee.** Clarendon, Tex. Clarendon Press. 1965.

Knyvett, William. "Battles of Dog Canyon", *Desert Magazine*, Palm Desert, Calif., April 1975.

McGraw, Kate. "Dog Canyon's Gritty Frenchman", *New Mexico Magazine*. March, 1975.

Sonnichsen, C.L. **Tularosa: Last of the Frontier West.** New York. Devin-Adair. 1960.

8

OPEN DOORS TO THE
SPIRIT WORLD

In New Mexico, any night can be Halloween.

This enchanted land has produced enough supernatural phenomena to fill a dozen books. It has had more haunted houses than New England, more witches than Salem and more ghosts than a Georgian swamp. Often, the Devil himself seems to have felt very much at home here.

It is impossible to cover all of the ghostly incidents that have occurred in New Mexico. Each of the state's three major cultural groups, the Indian, Spanish and English traditions, is steeped in its own distinct folklore of the supernatural. A few of the more curious and chilling tales are offered here, a mere sampling of the land's ghosts that seem as prevalent as the shimmering desert mirages on a scorching afternoon.

Obviously not all of these tales can be substantiated, but it is worth remembering that the New Mexicans who originated them swore the stories were true. While most of the stories are hair-raising, others, like the haunted rectory of Santa Cruz, are merely charming.

In 1798, a fine, sturdy church and convent were built in the fledgling settlement of La Villa Real de Santa Cruz, across the Rio Grande from Española. The rectory which accompanied the church was also a fairly impressive structure: two-stories, with several bedrooms, a large kitchen, dining hall and long corridors leading to storage rooms and closets. A single, narrow stairway led to the second floor where a comfortable drawing room had been furnished to accommodate weary travelers who stopped overnight in Santa Cruz.

In 1892, as the rectory neared its centennial anniversary, the pastor, Padre Halteman, was called to Santa Fe by the bishop. Before leaving, Father Halteman placed his housekeeper in charge. The true name of the housekeeper is unknown, but some have referred to her as Doña Teresa, a name as good as any at this point. She had a nine-year-old daughter, Tulitas, living with her in one of the rectory's many rooms. Down the hall, Santa Cruz's new school teacher, Doña Elenita, had recently taken up temporary residence.

Both Doña Teresa and Doña Elenita had been warned by the townspeople that the rectory had an odd and disturbing reputation. One of the early pastors, Fray Francisco, had met a violent death at the hands of marauding Indians. The successor, Fray Juan, had also died suddenly in a rather bizarre accident; he slipped and fell under the wheels of one of New Mexico's first trains.

After the death of the second priest, strange things began to happen in the rectory. Lights were seen passing by the upper windows at night and sometimes the back door was wide open the next morning. The parish sexton and gardener, old Gregorio, wouldn't go near the place after dark.

Doña Teresa was not a woman who could be easily intimidated; she was a hard-working woman, doing the best she could to raise her daughter. In short, she had no time for ghosts.

On that evening in 1892, with Padre Halteman off to Santa Fe, Doña Teresa bid the school teacher good night and blew out the candles after tucking little Tulitas into bed. She herself was just dozing off when she heard footsteps on the staircase, and heard the drawing room door open and close. She lay quietly in the darkness, listening intently. Although the floorboards creaked occasionally above her bed, she felt no sense of fear and soon fell asleep.

In the morning, she spoke to Doña Elenita about what she had heard. "It may have been a dream," she said, but Elenita shook her head. She, too, had heard the same sounds. Being practical, rather than frightened, they checked the rectory doors and found them all still securely locked. No one could have come in during the night.

That evening, Doña Elenita joined Doña Teresa and Tulitas in their room; the three waited quietly in the candlelight. Soon the footsteps ascended the stairs just as before, the drawing room door opened and closed, and the floorboards began to creak above their heads.

This time they listened even more intently and were able to discern some details they had missed before. It seemed obvious now that two figures had climbed the stairs, not just one, and that the creaking sounds seemed to be moving in some sort of irregular pattern, as if the persons were circling at frequent intervals.

Most curious of all, each time the footsteps halted, a soft click-clacking noise followed a few seconds later. Teresa and Elenita looked at one another in perplexity; they couldn't imagine what the strange noise could be.

During the remaining days of Father Halteman's absence, the ghostly ritual repeated itself nightly. Although Doña Teresa and Doña Elenita felt no fear about the eerie events, they still could not summon the courage to go upstairs and open the drawing room door.

When Father Halteman returned, they told him about the odd experience, describing the footsteps, the opening and closing of the door and the almost rhythmic pattern of the circling figures. Father Halteman furrowed his brow and nervously fingered his crucifix. He said he had heard these stories before from others who had stayed overnight in the rectory while he was gone. He could offer no explanation.

Continuing their story, the women tried to describe the peculiar click-clacking sound they had heard. It was then that Father Halteman's eyes opened wide. "So that's what it's all about!" he exclaimed. "That's why they keep coming back!"

He urged the women to come with him to the drawing room. Father Halteman fumbled with his large ring of keys and finally managed to open the long-locked door. He walked across the room, past the dusty chairs and sofas.

"This old parlor has provided rest and comfort for many a traveler," he said as he brushed a cobweb from his face. "But as you know, we don't get many visitors in Santa Cruz anymore. This room is no longer maintained."

He pointed to an object in the center of the floor. "That was always the parlor's principal attraction ... the billiard table. I don't approve of billiards myself; I consider it a frivolous game and a waste of precious time. That's why I keep this door locked, so others won't be tempted by it."

He ushered the women back through the doorway, closed and relocked the door. There was a tone of indignation in his voice when he said, "It appears, however, that Fray Francisco and Fray Juan enjoyed the game immensely. Ah, the nerve of those two! Every time I leave town, they sneak back in there to shoot pool."

Most of New Mexico's rather sizeable population of ghosts seem to be equally harmless, although some apparently seek more than recreation.

Another of New Mexico's early priests, Fray Juan F. Padilla, also met a violent death. Since his murder occurred in 1756, it is impossible at this late date to determine which account of his demise is correct ... or, indeed, if any account is accurate. He may have been slain by Indians near Gran Quivira or possibly, as another story says, he was "killed by stabbing thrusts" delivered by a jealous husband who mistakenly thought the good padre was his wife's lover.

How ever he might have died, it seems certain that he was buried in a shroud beneath the altar in one of New Mexico's oldest and greatest churches, the now ancient mission at Isleta Pueblo. There Father Padilla rested for nearly 20 years. Then in 1775, his body slowly rose through the hard-packed earthen floor.

Amazing as this phenomenon must have seemed to those who witnessed it, the condition of the dead priest's body was even more surprising. It had not decayed, was still soft and pliable, and had a pleasant earthy smell. No one who saw the corpse was frightened, so it is said, not even the children.

The parishoners speculated that the padre might be tired of sleeping in the bare ground, so they fashioned a coffin for him. It was a bit unconventional by today's standards, just a hollowed-out cottonwood log, but Father Padilla rested comfortably in it for the next 44 years.

Then in 1819, he rose through the floor again.

Fray Angélico Chavez, one of New Mexico's most superb historical researchers and a restorer of ancient churches, published an article in 1947 based on documents he had discovered in church archives which told of the investigation that took place after the 1819 resurrection of Father Padilla.

When the casket surfaced in the church floor, it was opened, and the body, now mummified, was examined. Church investigators could find no explanation of the floating coffin. An all-night wake was held and Padre Padilla was reburied.

Seventy-six years went by, during which a wooden floor was built into the old church. On Christmas Eve 1895, the restless padre made his most dramatic appearance. During the beautiful Indian dances that precede the midnight mass, Fray Padilla began knocking inside his cottonwood confinement. When he had gained everyone's attention, he shook the altar back and forth a few times.

The dancers were unnerved by the strange interruption of their celebration. The ceremony was halted to allow another investigation of Padre Padilla's whereabouts. When floorboards to the altar were pried off, the coffin was found to be out of the ground again, and pressing against the bottom of the altar.

In the presence of The Most Reverend Plácido Luís Chapelle, Bishop of Santa Fe, the casket was opened once more. The mummified body was examined by Dr. W.R. Tipton. Once again, no explanation could be offered. Padre Padilla was soon buried again, for the fourth time.

As an historian, Fray Angélico Chavez was also unable to provide a satisfactory solution to the mystery, even after an in-depth study of the records. He felt it was possible that the cottonwood coffin may have been bouyant enough that the shifting soil and sand beneath forced the casket up occasionally. But he admitted this would not account for the first appearance, when the padre was not in a coffin. Nor would it explain why the other caskets buried in the same floor never rose.

Perhaps Fray Padilla was restless because his life ended suddenly and prematurely; he may have felt his earthly work was unfinished. Whatever the reason, he seems to have resigned himself to retirement. After 230 years, he is apparently content to just lie there quietly and listen.

Not all of New Mexico's ghosts have been so fortunate. Some were destined to relive the most awful moment of their lives over and over until finally, the very place where they perished had ceased to exist.

In 1880, a little village sprang up along the pine-shaded banks of Bonito Creek on the eastern side of the impressive White Mountains, not far from present day Ruidoso. Settlers named the village Bonito City. It was an appropriate name, for the land around it was indeed very pretty. Folklorist Ted Raynor once wrote that the only law needed in Bonito City was the Golden Rule. That rule was said to have been obeyed unquestioningly by all its citizens.

It was a small town, nothing more than a few cabins, a couple of stores, one church, one saloon and a log hotel called The Mayberry. Hard to believe, then, that this pastoral spot became the scene of one of New Mexico's most grisly massacres.

On May 4, 1885, a lean, cold-eyed young man drifted into town. He was a total stranger to all, and he made no attempt to get acquainted. He registered at the Mayberry hotel as Martin Nelson. Later, he joined the other guests for supper in the hotel dining room. He spoke to no one, but watched them all with a serpent-like gaze. There was something about the look in Martin Nelson's eyes that made the other diners glance down and pay close attention to their plates.

After supper, the stranger returned to his room, and the other slightly unsettled guests retired for the night as well. After night fell, Bonito Creek continued to sing its cheerful, rippling night-song, but at 1:00 a.m., Martin Nelson rose from his bed. He carried his loaded rifle out into the hallway and knocked on the door next to his own. When the sleepy-eyed eldest son of the Mayberry family opened the door, Nelson shoved the rifle against the youngster's nightshirt and pulled the trigger. With hardly a pause, Nelson stepped into the room and shot the youngest boy as he sat up terrified in his bed.

At the sound of the shots, another guest, Dr. R.F. Flynn, rushed into the hallway. Nelson calmly turned and fired. Nelson moved on toward the top of the stairs in time to see the hotel's owner, John Mayberry, running up from below. Nelson killed him instantly with a bullet through the heart. Martha Mayberry, who had been following her husband, threw herself screaming on John's body. When she looked up, Nelson shot her almost point-blank. Streaming blood, she ran from the hotel and into the night. She was banging on the door of a neighbor's cabin when Nelson, who had stalked her slowly, walked up and fired the second and fatal shot.

Back at the hotel, the only surviving Mayberry child, Nellie, crept out the front door and made a dash for the forest. The killer saw her and took careful aim. His shot knocked the child head over heels into the bushes.

By this time, other townspeople had been aroused by the commotion. The grocer, Herman Beck, emerged from his cabin; Nelson dropped him with a single shot. The owner of Pete's Saloon sneaked up behind the killer, sprang on his back and tried to grab the rifle. He was no match for the blood-thirsty stranger, who simply flipped the bartender to the ground and drilled him with bullets.

Finally, Martin Nelson turned away and, with his rifle dangling loosely in his hand, slowly walked off into the woods.

The stunned citizens of Bonito City came warily out of their homes to survey the carnage. In less than 15 minutes, eight people had been shot. When they lifted little Nellie out of the bush, they realized she was the only victim still alive. Bringing rifles with them, they gathered in and around the village's largest cabins to wait out the long night. For the citizens of Bonito City, the night of May 5, 1885 must have seemed endless.

Finally daylight did come, and the dark forest became a soft, grey-green blur. Soon, sunlight and shadow etched in distinctive shapes of familar trees and rocks. It was a lovely spring morning, warm and sunny, fresh with the scent of ponderosa pine.

Then, Martin Nelson came walking back down the hillside, rifle in hand, and re-entered the town.

The men poised at the cabin windows, crouched alongside the nearby shed, cocked their weapons. When Nelson was close enough for them to see that unholy gleam in his eyes, they fired in unison. A dozen bullets struck the killer at once, jerking him off his feet and into the shallow water of Bonito Creek.

The dreadful episode had finally ended.

It took several days before the peace officers from Lincoln arrived to haul away Nelson's body. Nellie Mayberry was hospitalized and the seven victims were buried side by side in the tiny Bonito City cemetery.

No motive for Nelson's cold-blooded rampage was ever determined. Some folks speculated he was a prospector driven loco by loneliness, but others—those who had seen his eyes—had a more frightening theory. They believed he was no longer human when he checked into The Mayberry. They were sure his body was possessed that night, and that it was the Devil himself pulling the trigger.

A lot of people moved away after the killings and those who stayed behind avoided the deserted hotel. It wasn't long before eerie things began to happen in the once-idyllic Bonito City.

One morning, a small child came sobbing hysterically up from the creek where she had been playing. She said she had seen blood flowing in the water from the spot where Martin Nelson had died. That night, strange sounds emanated from the empty hotel; there were muffled shots that sounded more like echoes than distinct blasts, followed by moans and screams.

The blood-curdling phenonemon was repeated several times before townspeople mustered the nerve to go inside the abandoned hotel in the middle of the night. There, in the flickering light of their lanterns, they saw fresh blood glistening on the stairsteps, and heard blood dripping through the floorboards in the place where Dr. Flynn had died. In the morning when the townspeople returned, the blood was gone. After that, folks stayed clear away from the old hotel.

Bonito City continued its decline; gradually everyone moved away. The Mayberry hotel sagged and finally collapsed. In 1930, 45 years after the massacre, a dam was built across Bonito Creek. The waters of the reservoir rose and covered the haunted site, silencing the screams and moans forever.

If the Mayberry Massacre was perpetrated by the Devil, it was surely not his first appearance in New Mexico. Satan seems to have kept himself pretty busy in the mountains of northern New Mexico. Scores of tales of the Devil's work permeate the folklore of the mountain people.

One such tale recounts a horrifying incident said to have occurred near the town of Watrous. A young man, whose name no one remembers now, was riding his horse back into town late at night after having visited his cousin who lived on a farm several miles out in the countryside. The two youths had talked much longer than expected, and it was well past midnight when the fellow began his lonely ride back home. The road was a narrow dirt track with plowed fields on both sides; there was enough moonlight so that the horse was able to find its footing without stumbling. When the road wound its way through a grove of cottonwood trees, the rider heard a baby's cry.

He reined in his horse beneath overhanging branches, and listened. Sure enough, he heard the cry again. It seemed to come from the shadows near the earth-clutching roots of one of the giant cottonwoods. The young man dismounted and stepped cautiously through the roadside weeds until he found a tiny, sobbing infant lying on the ground, all alone in the dark, empty landscape.

Tenderly, he picked up the baby and carried it gently back to his horse. The horse's nostrils immediately flared, and it began stamping its hooves and shying away. The young man calmed the horse and swung carefully into the saddle with the baby cradled in his left arm. Grasping the rein with his right hand, he nudged the nervous horse onward.

He hadn't gone more than a hundred yards, when the baby looked up at him and said in an adult voice, "I don't like riding this way. Put me on the saddle behind you."

The young man was thoroughly astonished, but obeyed the baby's command to be placed on the cantle of the saddle. An odd chill passed through him as the baby gripped his waist with its little hands. By now, the horse was in a near-panic, snorting, blowing and side-stepping frantically. It was all the rider could do to control his mount. As he began to win back some control, he felt the hands on his waist grow larger.

The weight on his saddle grew heavier and a large form began rising behind him until it was pressing against his entire back. He heard a raspy, panting breath alongside his ear, and smelled a foul, nauseous odor. Still trying to rein in the horse, he glanced down to his waist and saw that the tiny hands had become huge, hairy paws. Terrified, he looked over his shoulder and saw a wild, hideous beast roaring in his face.

Half-human and half-panther was how the young man later described the creature. It had the ears of a bat and when it shrieked, the young man could hear the screams of all the tormented souls in hell.

The horse was now completely insane. While it reared and plunged, the rider threw himself from the saddle, tumbling into the roadside ditch. Badly stunned, he rose to his knees and crawled back on all fours to the edge of the road. Above him, an enormous, ghastly beast with long, tangled hair and a whip-like tail sat astraddle the bucking, leaping horse, lashing the poor animal to ribbons with its terrible claws. The screaming horse galloped madly down the road with the demon locked tight on its back, disappearing into the darkness.

The young man stumbled to his feet and began running in the opposite direction. Though it was several miles back to his cousin's house, he didn't stop until he fell against the door. His cousin responded, dragging him inside. The story told by the frightened young man was so incredible that probably no one would have believed him except for the jacket he wore. It had been shredded on both sides as he sprang from the monster's grasp. Needless to say, the horse was never seen again.

Other New Mexicans encountering the Prince of Darkness have not been so fortunate.

A strange tale shelved in the Folklore Archives of New Mexico Highlands University in Las Vegas apparently originated near the town of Cebolla. As always, this tale has been passed down from generation to generation; its origins may well be in colonial Mexico, rather than New Mexico, having traveled up the Jornada del Muerto with early settlers to this area. Regardless of its antiquity, it is a story that would have pleased Rod Sterling and his "Twilight Zone" writers.

It begins as a love story.

Antonio was in love with Lupita. He was from a poor family and she had been born rich. They had grown up in the same small village, but they were worlds apart. Antonio had frequently tried to speak to her when he passed her on the street, only to be rebuffed.

He often watched her from a distance, admiring her fine clothes, her long, velvet dresses with embroidered hems, her ruffled, freshly laundered blouses and the jaunty hats she always pinned at exactly the right angle on her perfectly combed hair. Then, he would look down at his own faded shirt and ragged pants.

When Lupita turned 17, her parents announced they would host a grand party at their hacienda. It was to be a masquerade ball; all who would attend were requested to wear costumes and masks. (Needless to say, Antonio did not receive an invitation.)

On the night of the ball, he sat morosely in his lonely room. The thought of Lupita dancing with all her other suitors was almost more than he could bear... until he suddenly had a brilliant idea. If he could rent a costume and mask, he, too, could go to the ball. No one would know who he was. He could mingle with the other elegant guests, dance with Lupita and be so charming that she would fall in love with him. At midnight, when the masks were removed, Lupita would realize that the man to whom she had given her heart was Antonio.

Inspired, he dashed from his dingy room to run to the shop where costumes were made, and caught the shopkeeper moments before closing. Antonio quickly selected an elegant black suit with a cape. He asked for a mask to go with it.

"The masks are all gone," the shopkeeper lamented, spreading his hands in sympathy.

Antonio looked frantically around the store. "What about that one?" he asked, pointing to a mask hanging in a dark corner at the rear of the shop.

The shopkeeper shook his head emphatically. "That mask is not for rent. There's something strange about it. I'm not sure what, but it frightens me."

Antonio walked over to the mask and peered at it closely.

Illustrator Herschel Caldwell, who specialized in southwestern themes, once produced a pen-and-ink sketch of the very mask in question, based on various descriptions of it. The archives at Highlands University include the sketch, showing that the top of the mask looked like a cow's skull; the slots for the eyes were narrow slits. There was a sharp, thin mustache above a wicked, fang-toothed grin, and it had a long, pointed goatee.

"I'll take it," Antonio insisted, pulling it down, "no matter what it costs."

Right in the shop, he dressed himself in the fine black suit, carefully adjusted the cape, placed the mask over his head and swirled off excitedly. His confidence seemed to rise almost immediately; minutes later he strode with a sense of assurance into the lavish ballroom. Other guests paused in their conversations; the ladies' fans stopped fluttering and the gentlemen raised their eyebrows nervously.

Antonio walked with a grace and ease he had never felt before in his life. Through the mask's eye slits, he searched the glittering salon for the lovely Lupita.

In spite of the masks, he had no trouble recognizing her. Although she wore a light blue, silken mask over her eyes, her beauty was unmistakable. In an almost dream-like state, Antonio walked toward Lupita. But her father stepped in front of him.

"I don't know who you are," Lupita's father challenged, "but stay away from my daughter." He took Antonio by the arm and ushered him out onto the patio.

"I only want to talk to her," Antonio pleaded. "And to dance with her."

"That," the old man replied, "is impossible. She is engaged to be married."

All of Antonio's new-found confidence drained away. He felt cold and empty. Then a fiery rage ignited within the lovesick youth. He grabbed Lupita's father by the throat, threw him down on the flagstones and broke his neck as if it were a twig. Several people who had been watching the confrontation from the doorway began to scream and shout.

Antonio fled into the garden and vaulted over the high adobe wall as easily as a bat would fly over it. With the cape flowing out behind him, he ran swiftly through the darkness and into a nearby grove of trees. There he pulled the hideous mask off his head and, gasping and panting, scratched a hole in the ground to bury the mask with dirt and leaves. He pulled a log over it before running in a crouch from shadow to shadow until he reached his home.

By now, the horrified party guests had recovered from their shock sufficiently to organize an impromptu posse. All of the village's streets were searched. They finally thought to arouse the shopkeeper from his sleep, and from him they learned who had rented the striking mask. They knew then that Antonio was the killer.

A large group of armed men rapidly surrounded Antonio's hovel. Four of the more courageous vigilantes stomped up to the door and pounded their fists. When no one answered, they broke down the door and burst into the room. What they saw froze them in their tracks.

He was standing motionless in front of his dresser mirror, gazing in horror at his reflection. His face had turned into an identical image of the mask he had torn off and buried beneath the cottonwood trees.

The original mask is said to be still out there somewhere buried under a few inches of dirt, awaiting its next obsessive wearer.

HOW TO GET TO THE FLOATING COFFIN OF PADRE PADILLA

While it is impossible to visit the site of some of the ghost stories mentioned in this chapter, one can easily travel to the church where Padre Padilla's corpse repeatedly rose from its grave. Drive 12 miles south from Albuquerque to Interstate 25 Exit 209. Turn off and drive to the northern part of Isleta Pueblo where St. Augustine Church dominates the plaza. The church was built in 1613, and was already 143 years old when Padre Padilla was buried ... first buried ... there.

BIBLIOGRAPHY

OPEN DOORS TO THE SPIRIT WORLD
Chapter Eight

Bullock, Alice. **Living Legends of the Santa Fe Country.** Denver, Colo. Green Mountain Press. 1970.

Chavez, Fray Angélico. "The Mystery of Father Padilla", *El Palacio.* November 1947.

Espinosa, Gilbert. **Heroes, Hexes and Haunted Halls.** Albuquerque, N.M. C. Horn. 1972.

Prince, L. Bradford. **Spanish Mission Churches of New Mexico.** Cedar Rapids, Iowa. The Torch Press. 1915.

Raynor, Ted. **The Gold Lettered Egg.** El Paso, Tex. Superior Printing. 1962.

Sherman, James and Barbara. **Ghost Towns and Mining Camps of New Mexico.** Norman, Okla. University of Oklahoma. 1975.

Simmons, Marc. **Yesterday in Santa Fe** Cerrillos, N.M. San Marcos Press.

9

NEW MEXICAN WITCHES
RIDE FIREBALLS

Witchcraft has been an important facet of the rich cultural traditions of New Mexico since very, very ancient times. Sorcerers who acted as conduits for spirits from the dark side of nature have been an integral part of Native American folklore for thousands of years.

In the complex Creation Myths of the Navajos, two deities, First Man and First Woman, controlled all witchcraft. When the Navajos made their long and hazardous journey up from their subterranean early worlds to the sunlit land they now inhabit, witches were ever-present. During the legendary passage, First Man and First Woman warned the people that, if they sinned, they could be punished by the witches.

Since witches are capable of shooting evil into a person, very serious diseases can be incurred. Once a Navajo has been stricken ill by a witch, elaborate ceremonies are needed for a cure. One of the best remedies is a ritual sweating which will purify the patient and

cause the invisible arrows and witch-objects to fall out
of the flesh. All too often, the intensive purging in
sweat-lodges is not enough; special chants must be
sung to defeat the witches' evil.

Apache witches are similarly feared. Sometimes
their power is equal to, or greater than, that of the
tribal medicine man. It is hard even to identify a witch
since all have the power to transform themselves at
will into a bird or animal. Male witches are said to favor
changing into a coyote.

The concept of the were-coyote is one of the scar-
ier aspects of Indian folklore. In the Pueblo world, a
coyote can be either a witch or a witch's pet . . . or it
may contain the spirit of a dead person. Sometimes,
women unwittingly married were-coyotes and thus became witches themselves.

On the brighter side, it is reassuring to find that
New Mexico's state bird, the roadrunner, is aligned
with the forces of good. The spunky roadrunner, with
its speed and alertness, its strength, endurance and
courage, has earned well-deserved admiration. Any
bird willing to deliberately pick a fight with a rattle-
snake will not be intimidated by witches.

Early accounts of Pueblo funeral rites show that
roadrunner symbolism was used to protect souls of the
deceased from the depredations of witches. Roadrunner tracks were scratched into the earthen floor in a
"magic circle" around the body, forming a barrier that
totally confused and thwarted evil spirits or witches
lurking nearby.

Perhaps the only . . . and surely the earliest . . .
photograph ever snapped of a New Mexico witch occurred in 1885, when that well-traveled historian,
Charles Lummis, captured on film the Witches of San
Rafaél.

For those disbelievers who scoff at the idea of
witches and their powers, a quick perusal of the 1885
Charles Lummis photograph may be in order. It is a remarkable picture.

Three women known as the Witches of San Rafaél posed for Lummis in the doorway of their adobe home. The eldest was Antonia Morales. She wore a shawl around her shoulders, held an ax in her knarled hands, and had turned her eyes away from the camera. Behind her stood her sister, Plácida Morales; she had drawn her dark cloak over her head until it covered most of her face. She was staring at the ground.

The third woman was Villa Morales, Plácida's 17-year-old daughter. Villa also wore a shawl, but it was a curious one. It had strips of cloth sewn around it and, though the photograph is grainy, there appear to be odd symbols on the cloth. Villa Morales was the only one of the three women who stared directly into Lummis' lens.

Her eyes were dark and narrow beneath sharply arched eyebrows. Somehow, she didn't look like your average teenage girl. Care should be taken in viewing the Lummis photo, however; one should not look too long into those haunting eyes of Villa Morales. It is said that her intense gaze once turned a man into a woman.

The Witches of San Rafaél were quite renown in their time. Their diabolical powers were so awesome that they were treated with considerable deference by their neighbors. Even so, they were definitely minor leaguers compared to the audacious episodes of New Mexico's more infamous witches.

New Mexico's first Hispanic witches had made a long journey even before reaching the Land of Enchantment. They came from Spain to colonial Mexico, and then on up the long oxcart trail, the perilous Jornada del Muerto. With them came an accumulation of wisdom and mystic powers that had already taken centuries to ferment and perfect.

Usually known as *brujas*, they were tolerated and even cautiously encouraged by authorities and socially prominent families because they possessed undeniable supernatural powers and talents that couldn't be obtained elsewhere. All agreed that the *brujas* were a source of mischief and considerable danger. But then, who else could instantly cure a migraine headache by passing an egg across the sufferer's forehead? Or dispell a serious illness by striking the patient's shadow with a broom? Or foretell the future with uncanny accuracy?

They were considered to have made pacts with the Devil to acquire their bizarre talents. People swore they had seen *brujas* turn a picture upside down just by looking at it, or make a pot boil by pointing a finger at it, or throw a rose through a windowpane without breaking the glass. People also knew that they themselves had sought the witch's assistance to produce a love potion, to disable a rival, or to communicate with a departed soul.

In New Mexican folklore, however, an important distinction is made between good witches and bad witches, or between *brujas* and *curanderas*. The latter follow a parallel line, separated from the *brujas* by the line between good and evil. *Curanderas* are gifted healers who may use mystical powers or native herbs and potent substances to relieve suffering and illness. Although the healer may have knowledge of the arts of witchcraft and often have psychic powers to predict the future, they invariably believe they were designated to use their special gifts to serve God by helping others. Their profound expertise in the use of herbs, curative teas, poultices, salves, incense and candles have earned them well-deserved respect and goodwill for as many generations as the *brujas'* arts have earned respect and fear.

The practitioners of *curanderismo* played very important roles in early New Mexico. Long before the discovery of penicillin, antibiotics and modern psychiatry, they were successfully curing physical aliments and alleviating mental distress through folk-healing and complex rituals. They performed their good works, then as now, with a selfless devotion to the people they served.

The *brujas*, on the other hand, use their powers for sinister purposes. If a witch performs a healing, one would never know the real reason for the service, or what price one might eventually have to pay.

On the dark side of witchcraft, suspicions linger long that the harm done—somewhere, sometime, to someone—in any ritual greatly outweighs whatever benefit may be achieved. *Brujas* constantly seek new recruits, so secret schools have sprung up time after time in all parts of the state.

Aurelio Espinosa, a turn of the century folk historian, once described a witches' school in a cave near Peña Blanca, some 50 miles north of Albuquerque. It was said the head instructor at that particular site was the Devil himself.

And where is the cave today, should one wish to verify its existence? It is gone, vanished, according to Espinosa. After the Devil's teachings were completed, both he and the cave completely disappeared.

A witch's apprenticeship is lengthy and pervasive. While mastering the art of the *mal ojo*, "the evil eye", to make a victim sick with a stare, the student witch also learns all there is to know about human greed. The witch learns about our desires for love and vengeance, health and wealth. She knows how to win our lover's devotion, how to destroy our rivals, and how to get even with those who slight or offend us. And most importantly, she learned just how high a price we are willing to pay for these ignoble acts.

New Mexican witches tend to ride fireballs, not brooms. They need only to clutch a pumpkin or gourd or even an egg to become airborne if they choose. Their ability to turn into owls is also useful for flight, of course, but their most spectacular means of aviation is simply to pop like a flashbulb and streak off in a fireball.

Throughout the years, countless New Mexico residents have seen luminescent globes flitting swiftly between the trees of darkened forests, or watched as balls of light, brighter than an arc-welder's spark, bounce over a suspected witch's home. Occasionally, a few brave souls have had the courage to approach one of these strange lights.

In the western foothills of Mount Taylor, Nicolas Marino saw such a fireball come down from the sky one evening. He watched it curve gracefully up through an arroyo. Nervously, he followed it, but when he was almost upon it, the light suddenly turned into a vicious snarling dog which sprang on him and then vanished after knocking him to the ground.

New Mexico's most famous witch is *La Llorona*, The Weeper. She is a nocturnal wanderer whose eerie wail has chilled the blood of New Mexicans for more than 200 years. Sometimes she cries and sobs, while other times, she shrieks and screams. But it is mainly that unearthly wail of hers that gives people the willies.

Different stories cite various reasons for *La Llorna's* eternal sorrow. New Mexico Historian Marc Simmons writes that there are no less than 42 versions of her story. Most often, it is said she was a widowed mother who drowned her children so she would be free to marry another man, who then rejected her.

Most folks say *La Llorona* can only be heard, never seen, but other people say they have, in fact, seen her late at night in the oldest parts of Santa Fe, dressed in black, dragging chains. She has never been known to enter anyone's home, but she will sometimes come up to a doorway to let out her lonely, pained wail. It is said she wants residents to know there will soon be a death in the household.

Another candidate for New Mexico's Witches Hall of Fame would be Doña Peipeiuta. She had a unique talent; she could take her body apart, limb by limb, and then put it back together again. María Candelaria Trujillo y Rudolph, a woman who lived in Lincoln County during the 1880s, said she had a great-uncle who had witnessed this feat firsthand.

Relating her uncle's story, María Candelaria explained her relative had snuck up to the window of Doña Peipeiuta's home in Lincoln County one evening. She already had a well-founded reputation as a witch by that time, so perhaps the great-uncle was exercising a researcher's curiosity rather than the more prurient art of the Peeping Tom. At any rate, when he peeked in the window, he saw Doña Peipeiuta sitting on a wooden bench in front of a steaming tub of water. First, she took off one of her legs, washed it in the tub and put it back on. She did the same with the other leg, and then plucked off her arms one at a time to rinse them thoroughly. Each time she plunged a limb into the tub, the water began to boil, the uncle reported.

It was not until she took off her head and scrubbed it vigorously that he fled.

Another Santa Fe witch of wide repute was Dolores la Penca. She lived alone on Agua Fría Road. For those who had the courage to seek out her services, one look around her mysterious home was enough to convince them they had come to the right place. Bundles of rare herbs hung from her rafters, medicinal plants grew in profusion on her window sills, and she always had vile-smelling pots simmering on her stove. Dolores la Penca's love potions and charms were highly-prized in the early days of Santa Fe, but her hexes and curses were even more respected.

Once, a young girl who lived in Dolores la Penca's neighborhood was being courted by two amorous young men. Eventually she chose one over the other, and the jilted loser sought help from the witch down the street.

Two days before the wedding, the bride-to-be broke out with the worst case of acne the town of Santa Fe had ever seen. Her entire face was suddenly covered with an ugly, lumpy, red rash that spread from her throat to her forehead. She looked so awful that it was decided the wedding would have to be cancelled.

That evening the girl's brother and a cousin were cutting firewood in the foothills when an owl flew in to perch in a tree above them. Both boys immediately felt a sense of dread.

"It's her," the cousin whispered. "It's Dolores la Penca. She's spying on us. Turn your back on her and do as I tell you. Take a bullet from your pocket. Carve a cross on it with your knife and load it in your rifle. Then, very quickly, turn back around and shoot that owl."

Nervously, the youngster followed his cousin's instructions. When he was ready, he took a deep breath, swung around, fired and knocked the owl out of the tree in a burst of feathers. When the boys picked up the dead bird, they found the bullet had gone directly through its right eye.

Back in Santa Fe, the bride's affliction cleared up within an hour. Her beautiful complexion returned and the wedding was held on schedule. Next morning, one of Dolores la Penca's customers entered her home to buy herbs and found the witch sprawled out dead on the floor . . . with a bullet wound through the right eye.

That story is similar to another originating in the Watrous area. Years ago, the town of Watrous was plagued by a slinking, black dog that came into town on moonless nights. The lean, haggard dog would savagely attack the local dogs, usually killing at least one. Then it would vanish into the night and not be seen again for another month.

Fed up with the periodic rampages that killed their faithful canine friends, the townsfolk vowed to do something about it. The next time the moon entered its darkest stage, several residents hid in the shadows to wait. Sure enough, the evil dog reappeared and they sprang on it, beating the culprit mercilessly with ax handles and chunks of firewood. They crippled the critter, but it got away yelping in pain.

When daylight came, the people of Watrous arose and went about their daily tasks. About midmorning, though, they noticed that the old woman who lived on the edge of town had not yet come out of her home. With neighborly concern, several villagers went by to check on her, only to find her lying in bed, bruised almost beyond recognition.

Of such coincidences are stories of witches made.

The life of a witch seems always to have been a risky one. Though her powers were great, a witch's occupation involved extreme hazards.

During the 1800s, two highly talented witches lived in "the oldest house in Santa Fe". For many years, they helped distressed Santa Feans solve their most difficult emotional problems. They dispensed both love potions and hexes, making a lot of local people fall in love and a lot of others fall dead. Then one night, a simple mistake put them both out of business.

As often happens, two young men had fallen in love with the same young woman. Each of them went to the Oldest House and bought a love potion . . . but the first fellow consulted one witch while the other, arriving later, made his bargain with the second woman. Neither witch was aware of the other transaction. The inevitable result of this confusion was that the young woman chose the man she would probably have wed anyway.

Greatly upset, the rejected suitor stormed into the witches' house and demanded that they change the young woman's mind. When they told him it was now impossible to meet that demand, the man struck the eldest witch and killed her. The second *bruja* grabbed a large knife and, with a single slash, decapitated the man who had murdered her sister.

Records do not say whether she was ever punished for beheading her client.

As tourist brochures in Santa Fe now proclaim, the Oldest House is now a curio shop. Nothing hints of its violent and bizarre past. However, some Santa Feans claim that occasionally, after the shop has closed for the night, the young lover's head bounces through the locked door and rolls off down the street.

A bad witch's skullduggery can usually be overcome by the workings of a good witch. An "evil eye" spell can be undone, hexes can be invalidated, curses neutralized by the use of herbs, holistic touching and perhaps trances.

Unfortunately, good witches are not always available when most needed. Frequently, therefore, New Mexicans have had to battle with evil witches on their own.

An oft-told tale of such an encounter originates in Las Cruces at an unspecifed time in the town's early history. The night watchman at the local lumber mill was found dead on the floor one morning when the mill foreman unlocked the door. The deceased watchman was a skinny little guy, but considered pretty tough. He had died without a mark on his body, in what remained a mystery.

A new watchman was hired; he, too, by chance was tough and wiry, and he, too, turned up dead the next morning. Suddenly job applicants were hard to find. At last, a soft, chubby sort of fellow accepted the watchman job. Though the mill foreman thought the new man was a little obese to be a good security guard, he handed him the keys, bid him good night and good luck.

About midnight, as the new guardian made his rounds, he was surprised to hear a sweet and seductive female voice coming through the keyhole of the main door to the mill. He listened closely as the voice softly asked him to let her come inside. His fat cheeks blushed red as she described the ecstasy they would share if he permittted her to come in.

The watchman, thinking of his predecesors, picked up an ax, braced his plump body against the door and opened it a crack. He asked the silky-voiced woman to extend her hand through the crack. When she did, he quickly traced the sign of the cross on it with his finger. The lovely voice immediately turned into an ear-splitting shriek. Instantly, the watchman slammed the door against the witch's wrist. Swinging his ax, he chopped off her hand.

The severed hand flopped about on the floor and

actualy tried to scuttle away as the horrified watchman kicked at it and stomped it. Within moments, the hand drew in its fingers and curled into a dried-up fist.

As brutal as the night watchman's reaction was, he may have saved himself from a very unpleasant fate: townfolks reckoned that his corpulent body might otherwise have become the main dish at a witches' feast.

Although most tales of New Mexico *brujas* are drawn from the early days, it should be remembered that witches are among us at all times. In the 1970s and 80s, bands of witches and their consorts gained some prominence in the Albuquerque and Santa Fe areas. Each spring, on the solstice, witches from central New Mexico gathered in the Sandia Mountains or other remote spots for well-attended rituals. Invoking the ancient powers of Wicca, these latter day witches are more apt to be Anglos rather than Indian or Hispanic, and may be dabblers in the occult, rather than deadly devotees of witchcraft.

Witches will forever be a part of the Land of Enchantment, plying their special art sometimes for good and sometimes for evil, but always with astonishing results. They give us brief glimpses of a shadowy realm that exists somewhere just beyond the limits of our comprehension about the natural world.

HOW TO GET TO THE WITCHES' HOME IN SANTA FE

Many of the homes of New Mexico witches no longer exist, either because they were burned by townfolks, or their unkempt, ramshackle abodes have long-since fallen into ruins. The home of two of New Mexico's most famous witches, however, is easily visited in Santa Fe, and can be included in a walking tour of the city's old churches. From the intersection of Old Santa Fe Trail and De Vargas Street, where San Miguél Chapel is located, stroll east from the chapel on De Vargas. The "Oldest House in the United States", formerly a witches' workshop, will be on your left.

BIBLIOGRAPHY

NEW MEXICAN WITCHES RIDE FIREBALLS
Chapter Nine

Bourke, John Gregory. **The Medicine Men of the Apaches.** Glorieta, N.M. Rio Grande Press. 1983.

Branch, Louis Leon. **Los Bilitos.** New York. Carlton Press. 1980.

Brown, Lorin W. **Hispano Folklife of New Mexico.** Albuquerque, N.M. University of New Mexico Press. 1978.

Bullock, Alice. **Living Legends of the Santa Fe Country.** Denver, Colo. Green Mountain Press. 1970.

Campa, Arthur L. **Hispanic Culture in the Southwest.** Norman, Okla. University of Oklahoma. 1978.

de Aragon, Ray John. **The Legend of La Llorona.** Las Vegas, N.M. Pan American Publishing Company. 1980.

Ortiz y Pino II, Jose. **Curandero.** Santa Fe, N.M. Sunstone Press. 1980.

Padilla, Floy. **New Mexico Folklore Record.** Albuquerque, N.M. Folklore Society. 1947.

Reichards, Gladys A. **Navaho Religion: A Study in Symbolism.** New York. 1950.

Simmons, Marc. **Witchcraft in the Southwest.** Cerrillos, N.M. Galisteo Press. 1968.

Torres, Eliseo. **The Folk Healer: The Mexican-American Tradition of Curanderismo.** Kingsville, Tex. Nieves Press. 1983.

Tyler, Hamilton A. **Pueblo Birds and Myths.** Norman, Okla. University of Oklahoma Press. 1979.

10
BILLY THE KID'S ESCAPE FROM THE GRAVE

The scene is the Maxwell Ranch near Fort Stanton, New Mexico. The date is July 14, 1881, and the time is near midnight. The young desperado enters the darkened bunkhouse. He pauses, sensing the presence of someone else in the room, someone he cannot see.

¿*"Quién es?"* he asks. Sheriff Pat Garrett, waiting in the corner, fires at the sound of the voice. Billy the Kid drops dead on the floor.

An old Navajo woman, Delvina Maxwell, who loved Billy like a son, runs into the room and throws herself over the body, sobbing. Garrett rises from his corner, holsters his pistol and walks off into the folklore of the Old West.

The death of Billy the Kid has fascinated the American people for over a century. Almost as a ritual, the fatal shooting of the West's most famous outlaw is reconstructed time and again, at movie houses and at "Old West" pageants. Cowboy movie star Johnny Mack

Brown strapped on Billy the Kid's guns in 1930. During the 1940s, a whole series of veteran B-Western actors, including Bob Steel, Buster Crabbe and Red Barry, portrayed the legendary outlaw. Roy Rogers played his only death scene as Billy, and even Audie Murphy couldn't survive Pat Garrett's fatal shot.

In all, no less than 38 films have been made about Billy the Kid. Pat Garrett shot Paul Newman in 1958, blew away Kris Kristofferson in 1973, and tracked down Emilio Esteves in 1988. There was even a 1966 film titled, "Billy the Kid vs. Dracula" . . . the one time that Billy won.

Obviously something about the Billy the Kid legend dies hard. Composer Aaron Copeland wrote a ballet about Billy in 1938; the star-crossed outlaw dies onstage accompanied by an immortal musical score. No less devoted to remembering the celebrated death is the town of Lincoln, New Mexico, where a Billy the Kid pageant is staged every August.

Billy the Kid, the West's most romanticized outlaw/folk hero, was shot dead by Patrick Floyd Garrett on the night of July 14, 1881.

Or was he?

The oddest aspect of the legend of Billy the Kid is that the Kid had a funny habit of showing up every so often after his death. At least, a lot of people swore that he did.

Proponents of the "Billy-Didn't-Really-Die" school of thought begin their arguments by pointing out the conversation that took place between Sheriff Garrett and his deputies immediately following the famous shooting.

Garrett's deputies, John Poe and Thomas McKinney, had been hiding in the shadows of the bunkhouse porch, waiting as back-ups in case Billy made a run for it. The exact wording of the conversation that night varies in each of the scores of books written about that fateful night, but the essential content is always the same.

"I got him, boys. I shot the Kid," said Garrett. But the deputies who had seen the figure cross the porch and enter the bunkhouse replied: "We think you shot the wrong man, Pat."

Even Garrett's autobiography confirms that his deputies expressed "their suspicion that I had shot the wrong man." Some accounts say Garrett was afraid to re-enter the bunkhouse to see who he had really shot. In any event, the body was examined that night and declared to be that of William H. Bonney, alias Billy the Kid.

Delvina Maxwell ordered Billy's body laid out on a carpenter's table. She placed lighted candles around him. The next day, he was buried in a grave which remained obscure and unattended for many years. The Kid was dead, but his legend took on a life of its own.

Some 20 years later, around the turn of the century, an odd sort of fellow came to New Mexico. His name, according to Southwest Author J. Frank Dobie, was "Walk-along Smith".

If a movie had ever been made about Walk-along Smith, Gary Cooper would have been the ideal actor to play the role. Walk-along was a man of few words, a loner, a wanderer. He never stayed long in one place, but he seemed to have been welcomed wherever he went.

He would show up, always on foot, at distant ranch houses. He earned his board and room by teaching the ranchers' children to read and write. But when he got the urge to move on, he would usually leave without a word.

Folks used to worry about him. He carried no baggage, and often didn't even have a canteen as he strolled off to the far horizon. But he always had a couple of books, a dog-eared writing tablet and a few pencils. He was often seen around Santa Fe, browsing through the shelves in the historical section of the library. When winter came, he headed south to the state's warmer regions, often to Reserve or Silver City.

There, it was said, he made a subsistence living giving piano lessons.

Those who knew Walk-along Smith fairly well said he was a gentle man, a kind-hearted soul who loved animals and children and, they emphasized, he would never touch a gun.

As the years went by, Walk-along was sometimes found by horsemen out in the backcountry, nearly dead from thirst. More than once, early automobile drivers found him lying in a roadside ditch. Many who recognized him were surprised that he lived as long as he did; it was 1937 before he passed away. His body was discovered near the Big Burro Mountains northeast of Lordsburg.

Now that he was dead, the backcountry ranchers who had known him for years felt it was safe to reveal Walk-along Smith's well-kept secret.

Ranchers came forward to say that the old man was none other than Billy the Kid. They said he had confided in a few friends about his real identity and had sworn them to secrecy. Walk-along Smith had described to them an elaborate plot concocted by himself, Pat Garrett and Territorial Governor Lew Wallace. Delvina Maxwell would also have had to be party to the deception.

According to the now-deceased wanderer's story, Governor Wallace and Sheriff Garrett, among many others, realized that Billy the Kid had been forced into his role as gunslinger during the vicious Lincoln County War. He had fought and killed only to defend himself, avenge his friends or escape the gallows.

There's no disputing the fact that Governor Lew Wallace was a romantic . . . he was writing *Ben Hur* at the time. Garrett was said to have convinced Wallace that William Bonney deserved another chance at life, that the notorious Billy the Kid might actually have a great potential for doing good.

With that agreement struck, a shoot-out was staged at the Maxwell Ranch. Two sacks of sand were buried in an unmarked grave to give the appearance of

Billy's demise. For his part, Pat Garrett collected the $500 reward from the governor, and Billy was sent off incognito to a prestigious university back east. Twenty years later, the outlaw returned as "Walk-along Smith".

The ranchers who told and re-told this tale could offer no real substantiation for their stories; they simply believed Walk-along was sincere when he told them he was really Billy the Kid. Nevertheless, many parts of Walk-along's story do coincide with the facts.

Walk-along played the piano and so did Billy the Kid. When Billy was on the run, he often sought refuge at remote rancher's homes. He repaid his hosts for his meals by playing the piano for them. It is also an established fact that Billy clandestinely met with Governor Lew Wallace in March 1879, and that the governor offered the Kid a deal. If Billy would agree to testify against the men who murdered Huston Chapman, Governor Wallace promised,"I will let you go scot free with a pardon in your pocket for all your misdeeds."

On March 21, 1879, Billy was arrested and thrown in jail in Lincoln. That night, Lew Wallace stood on the edge of the plaza, watching enthralled as the villagers gathered in front of the jail to play guitars and serenade the youthful outlaw in his cell. A few days later, Wallace wrote to the U.S. Secretary of the Interior in Washington, D.C. telling about "a precious specimen named the Kid . . . an object of tender regard."

However, as an appointed governor in frontier New Mexico, Wallace soon learned he lacked the political power to pardon an enemy of the infamous group of Republican lawyers, legislators and businessmen known as the "Santa Fe Ring".

It was also well known that Pat Garrett was a personal friend of the Kid for at least two years before he finally pinned on a badge and set out to hunt the outlaw down.

Could it be that both Wallace and Garrett actually cared enough about the charismatic young outlaw that they illegally arranged for his escape and disappearance? Billy, Garrett, Wallace, Delvina Maxwell and

Walk-along Smith are all long-since departed, so the true story will never be told by them. The ranchers who knew them personally are also deceased. One thing certain remains: there has never been a shortage of people who swore they had seen the Kid after his "death".

A Lincoln County pioneer woman, Mrs. J.H. Wood, told her grandchildren she had served Billy the Kid supper at her home on July 17, 1881. Mrs. W.W. Carson, a retired school teacher, recalled having met Billy in the spring of 1888 or 1889, when he helped her lead her frightened horse across a river. He was very kind, she remarked, a perfect gentleman. José Montoya, who as a schoolboy had watched Billy's escape from jail, saw the famous outlaw at a bullfight in Juarez in 1901. On June 27, 1948, the *El Paso Times* reported that one of Billy's friends, Manuel Taylor, ran across his old buddy in a cantina in Guadalajara in 1914.

To this day, some researchers swear that William Bonney changed his name to John Miller and lived out his life on a remote ranch near Ramah, New Mexico, in McKinley County. Billy the Kid was also seen in Duncan, Arizona, Mora County, New Mexico, and was once spotted running a restaurant in California.

The only problem with any of these accounts is that they were all "take my word for it" type stories . . . none of them carried any substantiation. Why would anyone believe Billy the Kid was still alive when they themselves had not seen him? Finally, one day in 1950, a real live, flesh-and-blood Billy the Kid walked onto the scene for all to see if they cared to.

In November of that year, New Mexico Governor Thomas Mabry received an unusual request from a law firm in El Paso, Texas. The letter informed the governor that the firm was acting as legal representative for a William V. Morrison who was seeking a pardon for a man who claimed to be Billy the Kid. The claimant, who called himself Billy Roberts, was asking for a full and complete pardon so he could "die a free man."

Governor Mabry was skeptical, to say the least. He replied that he would take no action on the pardon request until he had met and personally interviewed Billy Roberts. The governor invited Roberts and his attorney to visit the executive mansion on November 30, 1950.

In the meantime, Mabry assembled a formidable group of historians and journalists to be present for the interview. Pat Garrett's sons, Oscar and Jarvis, along with historical journalists Will A. Keleher, J.W. Hendron and Will Robinson, were seated with the governor when the ancient Billy Roberts entered the room. He was wearing a yellow buckskin jacket, a bright green bandana around his neck, and an enormous cowboy hat on his head. He balanced himself on a walking cane.

Billy Roberts was accompanied not by an attorney, but by a friend. It may well be that the initial letter to the governor was all the legal help that the old man could afford.

His friend, William V. Morrison, introduced himself as a member of the R.F. Robert accounting agency of Beaumont, Texas. He said his employer once introduced him to a distant relative, Billy Roberts. A series of converstions with this colorful old gentleman had convinced Morrison that the man was, indeed, the historical figure he claimed to be.

Morrison explained he had once been an investigator for a legal firm, and that by using his expertise in that field, he had sought verification of Billy Roberts' claim. He had interviewed scores of elderly people who had known Billy the Kid; most, though not all, had signed affidavits attesting that, after having met Billy Roberts, they believed his claim was authentic.

"This man is not an imposter," Morrison stated flatly. "He is the real Billy the Kid."

Billy Roberts then told his story to the governor and historians gathered in the New Mexico executive mansion. He said he was 91 years old, and that back in

1881, he was cowboying for a Lincoln County rancher, John Chisum. He had a saddle pal named Billy Barlow.

"Me'n Billy Barlow was just like two peas in a pod," Roberts told the gathering. "You couldn't hardly tell us apart."

On the fateful night of July 14, 1881, Barlow had been drinking heavily, and wanted to go over to the Maxwell Ranch to get some steaks. Billy the Kid was against it. He knew Garrett's posse was looking for them, probably at the ranch. Barlow insisted, and although he feared a trap, Billy (the Kid) Roberts said he accompanied his drunk friend. At the ranch, Barlow walked into the bunkhouse and Garrett shot him in the darkened room.

When Billy the Kid heard the shot, he raced toward the bunkhouse, but someone fired at him from the porch. The bullet creased his head and knocked him out. When he came to, he was lying in an adobe shack behind the main house, being treated by Delvina Maxwell, while Barlow's body was being laid out in the carpenter's shop.

Regaining consciousness, the Kid staggered to his feet, drew his pistol and headed for the door, ready to take on Garrett and his posse. At that moment, Celsa Gutierrez, one of Billy's sweethearts, burst into the room and begged him not to go out. She told him Garrett had realized he shot the wrong man and was now passing Barlow's body off as that of the Kid.

Recounting his tale to Governor Mabry, Billy Roberts went on to say that at 3:00 a.m. that night, in the early hours of July 15, his girlfriend brought a horse up behind the adobe shack, gave him a quick goodbye kiss and sent him off into exile.

Billy Roberts said he took refuge in sheep camps for several days and eventually reached El Paso with the help of friends. He crossed the Rio Grande and went to hide in Chihuahua for the next two years.

Wrapping up his story, Roberts removed his great sombrero to show the governor the deep scar on his balding head. Then he leaned back in his chair to field questions from the skeptical historians. They tore into him, grilling the old man about the Lincoln County range war and the gunfights at Mockingbird Gap and Stinking Springs. They asked for details about the men he had ridden with or ridden against.

Old Billy Roberts held his own pretty well for a 91-year-old codger discussing events that had occurred 70 years earlier, but there was an awful lot that he didn't remember. Or didn't know. His memories of the shootout at Blazer's Mill and the seige of the McSween house were vivid and accurate, but on many other points, he seemed vague and confused.

"Seventy years is a lot to recollect, Governor," he said during the interview.

At the end of the grilling, the Garrett brothers, the reporters and the historians dismissed Roberts as "the victim of a delusion". Governor Mabry declared he would not take action on the application for a pardon for Billy the Kid. William Morrison helped his aged friend out the door of the mansion and into their car. They drove back to Albuquerque to spend the night in a cheap Central Avenue motel. Next morning, they read the derisive articles about them in the *Albuquerque Journal*, and headed back to Texas.

It may well be that Billy Roberts was a self-deluded man and that Morrison's faith in the old man's story was based more on affection than fact. But several aspects of this curious episode cannot be ignored. First of all, the "experts" who cross-examined him made more mistakes than Roberts did.

The *Journal* misspelled the name of the famous John Chisum, calling him "Chisholm". The newspaper also stated melodramatically that the real Billy the Kid had "died with his boots on. . . . " All accurate historical accounts confirm that the man shot as Billy the Kid that night had actually pulled off his boots and was walking in stocking feet when he was shot. And according to the *Journal*, the Kid shot three guards during his escape from the Lincoln County Courthouse, when in reality, two guards were shot.

As for the other experts, the historians with Governor Mabry also erred in their version of the "real Billy the Kid". They asked Roberts where he was born. Roberts answered, "Buffalo Gap, Texas."

The historians scoffed. They said it was "a well-documented fact" that Billy the Kid was born in New York City. Yet the best researcher on Billy the Kid, Jon Tuska, has since written that, although it cannot be determined where the Kid was born, it definitely was *not* New York. His mother never lived there.

Another common misconception surfaced during that 1950 interview in Santa Fe. The historians made much of the fact that Billy Roberts was right-handed. They said everyone knows the Kid was left-handed. They were wrong again. The myth of the "left-handed gun" arose, according to Tuska and many other researchers, because a famous photograph showing the Kid wearing his revolver on his left hip was a tintype that had been reversed. Other photos of Billy the Kid clearly show him with his pistol on the right.

William Morrison doggedly pursued his interest in Roberts' claim. A couple of years after the failed interview with the governor, Morrison made an astounding discovery. Aided by another researcher, prominent Southwest Author and Historian C.L. Sonnichsen, they found proof that supported the old man's version of the life of Billy the Kid.

Morrison and Sonnichsen were comparing photographs of Billy Roberts and Billy the Kid, paying close attention to the ear shape in each of the old photographs. Human ears are almost as unique as fingerprints, physiologists have concluded; two pair of ears are rarely exactly the same. In their comparisons, Morrison and Sonnichsen found that the ears of Billy Roberts and William H. Bonney were identical.

HOW TO GET TO THE GRAVE OF BILLY THE KID

The grave of Billy the Kid and the Billy the Kid Museum are located at 1601 E. Sumner Avenue in Fort Sumner, 44 miles southwest of Santa Rosa on U.S. Highway 84. These sites have been the town's number one tourist attraction for as long as anyone can remember.

The Kid's original tombstone was stolen, and has since been replaced. It is protected by a cage of iron bars, making it appear that Billy the Kid has been jailed forever. The inscription reads: "The Boy Bandit King. He Died As He Had Lived." Decide for yourself whether the inscription is true.

BIBLIOGRAPHY

BILLY THE KID'S ESCAPE FROM THE GRAVE
Chapter Ten

Adams, Ramon F. **A Fitting Death for Billy the Kid.** Norman, Okla. University of Oklahoma. 1950.

Albuquerque Journal. November 30, December 1, 1950.

Branch, Louis Leon. **Los Bilitos.** New York. Carlton Press. 1980.

Dobie, J. Frank. **Apache Gold and Yaqui Silver.** Boston, Mass. Little, Brown and Company. 1939.

Garrett, Pat. **The Authentic Life of Billy the Kid.** Albuquerque, N.M. Horn and Wallace (Reprint). 1964.

Smith, Wilber. "The Amigo of Billy the Kid", *New Mexico Magazine.* April, 1933.

Sonnichsen, C.L. and Johnson, William V. **Alias Billy the Kid.** Albuquerque, N.M. University of New Mexico Press. 1955.

Tuska, Jon. **Billy the Kid: A Bio-Bibliography.** Westport, Conn. Greenwood Press. 1983.

11

TEN MILLION BUCKS
IN THE BOOTHEEL

No one knows who dug that hole out there in Skeleton Canyon.

Most likely, it was a couple of small-time prospectors who had hit a little stringer of gold and followed it until it pinched out at a disappointingly shallow level. They probably made a few dollars for their trouble before they loaded up their burros and roamed onward. Likely, they never gave a second thought to the shaft and pile of dirt they left behind.

Maybe they struck it rich further down the road; maybe not. Luck is fickle, but there's one sure thing about that hole in southwestern New Mexico; if they had known how rich their little abandoned mineshaft would eventually become, they wouldn't have wandered off forgetting it.

Apparently, they never even bothered to file a claim on their modest diggings there, for no records show its location. If there were records of any kind, someone might be able to relocate the site and recover the $10 million worth of gold, silver and historic artifacts that have been buried in that mineshaft for well over a century.

The mineshaft is located somewhere in the least-known, seldom visited part of New Mexico, in that little southwestern tip of the state known as the Bootheel. Bordered on the south by Mexico, on the west by Arizona and pretty much ignored by everybody, it is the peculiar, squared-off jog on the map that constitutes the extreme southwestern corner of the state. Typical of land ownership patterns elsewhere in New Mexico, some of it is federal land and other parcels are private ranches. It's not a very big area, but it offers a sense of vastness, with its wide, empty openness uncorrupted by the 20th Century.

However, the story of the treasure in the Bootheel does not begin there, nor in the 20th Century. It starts in 1879, when two notorious gangs of outlaws sat down together in a border cantina to plot a robbery so audacious it would make Butch Cassidy and the Sundance Kid look like dime store shoplifters.

The first gang was called *Los Bandidos de la Estrada*, Bandits of the Highway, but more often referred to as the Estrada Gang. They were all Mexicans and had acquired a well-earned reputation for their daring methods of making bank withdrawals.

The other outlaws were less glamorous; they had simply christened themselves "The Hughes Bunch". Their name would hardly do for a movie marquee, but they were, in fact, five of the meanest villains that ever shot up a saloon. Their leader was an utterly ruthless man named Jim Hughes. Second in command was "Curly Bill", a deadly gunslinger who was so fast on the draw that he hoped to go up against Wyatt Earp someday . . . just for the fun of it. The other members of The Hughes Bunch were not exactly the nicest people drifting around New Mexico in those days either: "Doc" Neal, Zwing Hunt and "Sandy" King.

History books don't tell the names of the Estrada Gang, but they were probably about the same number as the Hughes gang. The main difference was that their leader thought big, really big. He had arranged the meeting in the cantina, and over a bottle of tequila, he offered Hughes a proposition.

First, he made an overture, suggesting, "You are wasting your time and talent, Señor Hughes, by robbing stage coaches. I think you are like me. You are destined for bigger things." Then he proceeded to tell Hughes about a plan he had conceived, a plot so bold that if it succeeded it would be the greatest robbery the West had ever known.

The leader of the Estrada Gang proposed that Hughes and his gang join forces to rob the Mexican government's mint in Monterrey.

Hughes listened to the details, and then he did something he had rarely done in his entire life. He smiled. The Mexican bandidos and the Anglo desperados raised their shot glasses and clinked a toast.

The first part of the operation was up to The Hughes Bunch. Mules would be needed to haul the loot. What better place was there to get good, well-fed, sturdy mules than the United States Army? It was child's play to steal 25 Army burros, which they quickly herded across the border. Next, they made a side trip to a Chihuahua bat guano mine where they loaded the mules with sacks of guano.

A few days later, posing as entrepreneurs in the fertilizer business, The Hughes Bunch drove their pack train down the narrow streets of Monterrey.

The Estrada Gang had arrived nearly a week earlier and had already begun putting their part of the plan in motion. They had struck up acquaintances with the small detachment of young soldiers assigned to guard the mint; the soldiers had been invited to come out to the Estrada camp on the outskirts of Monterrey for cards, tequila and other pleasantries when they went off-duty.

At first, just a few soldiers accepted the invitation, but they returned to tell their fellow-guards about the fine time they had had with their new friends. These were good-natured strangers, very generous with their tequila. They liked to laugh and smoke and gamble. And they were very good losers, too, which added to their appeal. Each of the visiting soldiers had won several hands of three-card monte, but the amiable strangers seemed to laugh all the harder when they lost.

In no time, the Estrada camp became a popular hangout for the *soldados* of Monterrey.

When Jim Hughes and his men got into town with the mules, the Estrada Gang made its move. They told the soldiers they would be leaving town soon, and wanted everyone to come out to the camp for one last party. All of the off-duty guards attended, and, if the truth were to be known, so did most of the sentries who were on-duty at the mint.

At the Estrada camp, they were greeted with tequila and laughter and *abrazos*. The leader of the Estrada Gang toasted everyone and asked who wanted to play monte. All of the young soldiers crowded eagerly around the blanket spread out on the ground. When the cards were dealt and all bets had been placed, the leader of the Estrada Gang rose to his feet and announced, in a nearly apologetic tone, "I am sorry, *mis amigos*, but this time, you lose."

The Estrada Gang quickly drew their pistols and fired away at the seated guests.

At the sound of the gunfire, The Hughes Bunch, stationed across the street from the mint, stormed the massive building, overpowering the few remaining guards. The captured soldiers were forced to open the heavy, wrought iron gates and the vaults. Then they, too, were shot.

Hughes' men emptied the sacks of bat guano on the ground and refilled them with armloads of gold bullion, silver ingots and huge bags of coins. The Estrada Gang rode up to join in the looting and help load the mules. So exhilarated were they with their success that they stopped to loot the magnificent cathedral of Monterrey as well, hauling off its priceless religious artifacts and a jewel-studded statue of the Virgin Mary.

The bandits drove their mule train out of town, taking advantage of a long headstart on pursuers dispatched from Durango. The gangs knew they had to cross the border again into U.S. territory as quickly as possible, but they also had to steer clear of Texas and New Mexico where the U.S. Army would be searching for the stolen mules. So they ran a northwesterly course across Chihuahua Province, into Sonora. Within a few days, they entered Arizona.

From there they probably followed the old Fronteras Road past the Pedragosa Mountains, and pitched camp somewhere in the White River basin.

Safely out of Mexico, the leader of the Estrada Gang suggested to Hughes that it was time to divide the loot and part company. Another of Hughes' rare smiles crossed his face. "It's already been divided," he said. "But only five ways."

Instantly, The Hughes Bunch went for their guns, shooting the startled Mexicans before they could react. With their former colleagues lying dead or dying around them, Hughes and his men finished their morning coffee before packing their gear. Mounting up, they led the heavily-laden mule train on into New Mexico's Bootheel.

No two historical accounts agree on how much loot those mules carried. Some say it was about $800,000, while others estimate it closer to a full million. Besides, who could put a monetary value on the jeweled holy statue of the Virgin?

Hughes knew right where to take his fantastic treasure. A year or so earlier, when he was on the run after a shoot-out, he had escaped from a pursuing posse by riding into the wild, uninhabited Peloncillo Mountains. He remembered that as he rode through Skeleton Canyon, he had passed a small abandoned mineshaft. He wasted no time in guiding the pack train to this ready-made treasure hole.

When the outlaws reached the mine, it was full of tumbleweeds. It only took a couple of matches to clear them out. After the bandits had stuffed their saddlebags full of silver coins, they dumped the rest of the Monterrey loot into the abandoned mineshaft. Then they filled the shaft with dirt, turned the mules loose to fend for themselves and rode north to Silver City.

They had gone without whiskey long enough and they were ready to celebrate.

The Hughes Bunch's Silver City binge was one the little town would not soon forget. The outlaws burst through the bat-winged doors of the town's best saloon, fired pistols into the ceiling and announced they were buying drinks for the house. All, except for Jim Hughes himself, proceeded to get gloriously drunk. The piano player was informed that there would be no intermission, and the bartender was told there would be no closing time. It was a grand night for The Hughes Bunch.

But they did have one problem on their hands . . . Doc Neal. Old Doc didn't drink any more than the rest of them, but he couldn't hold his liquor as well. Besides, he always tended to talk a little too much. By midnight, he had gathered a pretty good-sized audience around a corner table listening to his tale of a fabulous treasure he had helped bury in Skeleton Canyon.

Everyone was fascinated by Doc's story, especially one man known historically as "the easterner", who began to ask specific questions about the location of the treasure. Jim Hughes walked across the room, lifted Doc Neal out of his chair and slapped him a few times. Hughes shoved the drunken old man into Curly Bill's arms, ordering that he be dunked in a horse trough and put on a horse.

There was a grim expression on Hughes' face when he sat down in Doc's empty chair. He offered to buy the easterner a drink, but the tenderfoot nervously declined. To which Hughes is reputed to have responded, "Then I don't think you're man enough to live in New Mexico." Hughes drew his pistol, fired and the easterner hit the wall like a swatted fly.

The party was abruptly over. Hughes and his men raced out of the saloon to their horses and thundered off. A posse of outraged citizens was swiftly organized, setting off in hot pursuit. They rode throughout the night and caught up with the gang just at dawn. Overtaking Doc Neal first, the posse began shooting at him as they closed in. Doc was hit several times and fell dead from his horse.

Soon the posse was within range of the rest of the desperados. Blazing away again, they knocked Zwing Hunt out of his saddle, too. By then, Hughes realized he could not outrun the posse, so he reined in his horse in a cloud of dust, leaped to the ground and began to fire away at the armed men charging down on him.

The odds were about 20-to-one against him, but at least Hughes survived. He was badly wounded when he and Zwing Hunt were taken prisoners. Curly Bill and Sandy King managed to escape and rode on into Arizona.

Jim Hughes was tried and convicted of murder. He went to the gallows, while Hunt served a 30-day sentence for being drunk and disorderly. Once released, Hunt took off to find his pals. However, he made the mistake of crossing Apache territory; his body was not found for several weeks.

Over in Tombstone, Arizona, Curly Bill finally got his chance to take on the legenday Wyatt Earp. After Curly Bill was buried, Sandy King rode back to New Mexico.

Young Sandy King was now the last member of The Hughes Bunch, the only person still alive who knew where the treasure from the Monterrey mint was hidden. King didn't think he'd be too welcome back in Silver City, so he drifted farther south . . . to a new little town called Shakespeare.

Shakespeare, New Mexico, is a ghost town today, but in 1879 it was a pretty lively place. The population was just under 200, but the main street (called Avon Avenue, naturally) already had two hotels, an elegant saloon, a well-stocked general store, and several other solidly-built adobe structures. Sandy King apparently headed first to the saloon.

He proceeded to get outrageously drunk. Late in the afternoon, he staggered out into the street and practiced his fast draw by shooting out most of the town's windows. He stumbled into the general store, selected a fancy silk bandana, and held a quarter up in front of the clerk's face. When the clerk reached for the coin, King let it drop. The drunken outlaw drew his pistol and shot off the clerk's index finger before the quarter hit the floor.

Sandy King thought it was uproariously funny, but the good citizens of Shakespeare felt King was taking his frontier humor just a bit too far. They waited until he passed out, then threw him in jail.

In the Shakespeare lock-up, Sandy's cellmate was a man called "Russian Bill", a horse thief by trade. Stealing horses was a capital offense in those days, and Bill was scheduled to be hanged in the morning. The Shakespearean powers-that-be figured as long as they were having a hanging, they might as well include Sandy King and get rid of two nuisances at once.

There aren't any big trees around Shakespeare; just piñón and juniper country, so the necktie party had to be conducted indoors. Russian Bill and Sandy King were taken to the dining room of the Stratford Hotel where ropes were tossed over one of its sturdy rafters.

When King was asked to step up on a chair, he decided it was time to do a little plea bargaining. If the townspeople would spare his life, he said, he would lead them to an enormous treasure in Skeleton Canyon. Nobody believed him, so nooses were placed around the necks of the two lawbreakers. Townsfolks had themselves a swinging good time when the chairs were kicked out from under the two outlaws.

There are two versions of the aftermath of those executions. Some books say the bodies were removed right away so the cook could serve breakfast. Others claim Sandy and Bill were left hanging until the stagecoach pulled in later, so that a spectacle would be offered for the unsuspecting passengers who came in for dinner. Back in those days, nearly everybody had a bit of that frontier sense of humor.

As it turned out, Sandy King, the last of The Hughes Gang, unwillingly took the secret of the Monterrey treasure with him to his grave. It wasn't until later that folks in Silver City and Shakespeare learned that The Hughes Bunch had, indeed, hauled off most of the contents of the Mexican mint. A few townfolks believed that old Doc Neal and Sandy King might have been telling the truth after all about the mineshaft full of treasure in Skeleton Canyon.

Over the years, a lot of people went out to search in Skeleton Canyon, but they found nothing. Some folks began to wonder whether the drunken outlaws could have gotten the name of the canyon wrong; maybe it was Skull Canyon they meant. After all, Skull Canyon is located in the same mountain range as Skeleton Canyon. Or it could be Little Skull Canyon, which is just a couple of miles further north. Or Owl Canyon. Or Whitmore.

More likely than not, the treasure is still out there in the Bootheel. By now, a Madrean oak or a piñón pine must have spread its protective roots over the sacks of gold and silver, and the Virgin's jewels may have lost some of their luster, but it's sure to be worth even more than a million dollars today.

In 1879, the treasure was reportedly worth one million. Back in those days, when cowboys worked for

$40 a month, and miners were lucky to get a dollar a day, a million bucks was an awful lot of money.

Yet today the same loot would be worth vastly more. Ten million seems a very conservative estimate. Adventurous divers often go to the bottom of the ocean in search of treasures that immense. How much easier it would be to go out to Skeleton Canyon and shovel out a mere 20 feet of dirt covering the entrance to a mineshaft full of treasure.

HOW TO GET TO SKELETON CANYON

The Bootheel area is accessible via State Highway 338, which goes south off of Interstate 10, 12 miles west of Lordsburg. The first 30 miles are paved; then the road is gravel for the next 35 miles as it travels along the east side of the Peloncillo Mountains.

These mountains are cut by many canyons, seen from the road. Skeleton Canyon, Skull Canyon and its branch, Little Skull Canyon, are the last ones above the northern boundary of the Coronado National Forest. They are on private land, but once you reach the southern end of this narrow, vertical strip of national forest, six miles from the Mexican border, you can hike trails so beautiful you may forget all about the ten million bucks in the Bootheel.

BIBLIOGRAPHY

TEN MILLION BUCKS IN THE BOOTHEEL
Chapter Eleven

Crocchiola, Stanley Francis Louis. **Shakespeare: A New Mexico Story.** Pampa, Tex. Pampa Print Shop. 1963.

Jenkinson, Michael. **Ghost Towns of New Mexico: Playthings of the Wind.** Albuquerque, N.M. University of New Mexico Press. 1967.

Mitchell, John D. **Lost Mines and Buried Treasure along the Old Frontier.** Glorieta, N.M. Rio Grande Press. 1970.

Sherman, James and Barbara. **Ghost Towns and Mining Camps of New Mexico.** Norman, Okla. University of Oklahoma Press. 1975.

Varney Phillip. **New Mexico's Best Ghost Towns.** Flagstaff, Ariz. Northland Press. 1981.

12
MYSTERIES OF THE ANASAZI

From the air, the floor of Chaco Canyon looks like a place where a careless giant once casually tossed his broken pottery.

The great, wondrous ruins of Pueblo Bonito resemble half a bowl that was cracked and shattered when it landed at the base of a tall, sandstone escarpment. Nearby, the broken shell of Chetro Ketl, with its deep, round, secretive kivas, could have been half of an enormous candleholder. Pueblo Pintado's impressive remnants must have been flung over the giant's shoulder, for they lie out in the open, miles away from the other ruins.

To the northwest, where the canyon's long mesas claw at the land like the paws of sculptured Egyptian lions, nine more extraordinary ruins rise to form the most spectacular array of prehistoric stone villages in the United States.

These great pueblos have been deserted for nearly 800 years, but they stand today as awesome monuments to the people who built them. We refer to these bygone builders as "Anasazi", the Ancient Ones, and their achievements are mindboggling in their magnitude. They built massive structures during an age when most prehistoric southwestern people still lived in roofed pits. They used advanced, near-perfect architectural designs and flawless engineering. They created a sustainable way of life in a harsh, arid environment. To do all this while evolving a rich, distinctive culture was an accomplishment that only becomes more remarkable with the passage of time.

Construction of the great Chacoan pueblos was incredibly labor-intensive; the stone had to be hand-quarried, transported, shaped, mortared and set in place. To use the Chetro Ketl ruin as an example, an estimated 50 million pieces of sandstone were fitted for its construction. The structure has 18 kivas and subterranean chambers, so tons of earth had to be removed. The roof of the main chamber was supported by immense columns standing in masonry-lined holes beneath which four stacked sandstone slabs had been positioned. Each slab weighed over half a ton, and none has settled more than slightly since it was buried. Foundations securing the three-foot-thick walls have proven equally durable after 800 years.

As imposing as its stonework is, Chaco Canyon's utilization of pine logs was even more remarkable. Logs, many the size of contemporary telephone poles, were used as rafters, roof supports and reinforcing bars within the outer walls. Archaeologists have estimated that at least 200,000 were needed to build the major pueblos.

Somehow, a people who had never held a steel axe, and had never seen a horse or a wheel, managed to fell and hand-haul perhaps a quarter of a million trees from distant forests, the closest of which was 35 miles away.

The size of the Chacoan structures was unparalleled. One of the larger buildings in Chaco Canyon, Pueblo Bonito, covered three acres, stood four stories high and consisted of 800 rooms. As a 1920 National Geographic Society team noted, "No other apartment house of comparable size was known in America or the Old World until the Spanish Flats were erected in 1882 at 59th Street and Seventh Avenue, New York City."

The Anasazi were not just builders of massive housing projects. Equally marvelous were their artistic skills and their ability to create small, exquisitely delicate objects. Their pottery surpassed all other ceramic achievements among the prehistoric people of North America. On the highly-polished, white surfaces of their earthenware, they traced thin, black lines. Sometimes the brushstrokes were direct and linear, circling a vessel above a row of jagged lightning flashes, or framing a complex pattern of dotted squares, or stair-stepped triangles. Nature's creatures were frequent motifs: an alertly poised deer, graceful birds, and sunbathing lizards often appear in silhouette on the ivory-toned Anasazi pots.

Even household utensils made of bone were embellished with inlaid bands of tiny, matching bits of turquoise surrounded by rows of lustrous black jet and pink coral. Anasazi craftsmen valued turquoise very highly and worked the stone with skill and precision.

In 1921, Neil M. Judd, an archaeologist from the Smithsonian Institute, discovered a four-strand turquoise necklace in Pueblo Bonito. The necklace was composed of 2,500 tiny beads, each individually polished and drilled. The drill holes were so small that an ordinary needle would not pass through them; Judd was only able to re-string the beads using a banjo string borrowed from a fellow worker. Whoever originally wore that lovely necklace had a choice of two sets of earrings to go with it. Alongside the necklace lay four flawlessly smooth, rectangular, blue ear-pendants.

The Ancient Ones were constant sky watchers. They carefully tracked the position of the sun as it traveled between winter and summer solstices. This enabled them to accurately chart the cycles of the seasons; to know when to plant, harvest and schedule their ceremonies. To facilitate their observations, they devised many ingenious solar timepieces.

Above a ledge on a canyon wall near the ruin of Wijiji, a white sun symbol was painted on the rock. If one stands at this spot at dawn on the day of the winter solstice, the sun will rise from behind a tall, rock pillar on the southeastern horizon. When the sun sets that same day, it will disappear into a V-shaped notch in a cliff to the southwest. Whoever first discovered this perfect solar marker was surely a genius.

Windows of the great Chacoan buildings were also used as solar markers. In the above-ground part of the great kiva of Casa Rinconada, there is a small east-facing window which lets in the first rays of dawn. On the opposite wall, small niches have been built in seemingly inexplicable patterns. But on the morning of the summer solstice, dawn's light moves down the wall and illuminates one specific niche, announcing with a glowing luminescence the coming of a new season.

Most fascinating among the many solstice markers of Chaco Canyon is the hauntingly beautiful Sun Dagger of Fajada Butte. Near the top of this tall, sharp mesa that stands at the entrance to the canyon, three large stone slabs lean against the sandstone wall. Two of the slabs are pressed so close together that only a thin, vertical sliver of sunlight can pass between. Behind the tilted slabs, a spiral petroglyph has been pecked into the wall at the precise location where, on the summer solstice, a tiny knife-blade of light shines across the exact center of the spiral.

The night sky and phases of the moon were undoubtedly of equal importance to these remarkably perceptive people. In the year 1054 A.D, a brand new "star" suddenly appeared in the constellation Taurus. This stellar explosion was a supernova whose remnants are believed to have formed the Crab Nebula. The supernova was so brilliant that it was visible in the daytime for 23 days before it began to fade. It was at its brightest on July 4, 1054, at which time it could be sighted just two degrees from the moon's crescent.

In a sky filled with millions of stars, most ancient people probably did not notice the appearance of one more pinpoint of light. But Chinese astronomers recorded the supernova event, and so, apparently, did the Anasazi.

Under a stone overhang beneath the Peñasco Blanco ruin, three symbols are painted in red pigment. The first symbol is the spread-fingered imprint of a human hand. This marks the site as a sacred one. Below the handprint is an upside-down crescent moon, and alongside the moon is a ten-pointed, asterisk-shaped symbol which many archaeologists believe may well be a depiction of the supernova. They believe it is more than coincidence that a star symbol was painted next to a moon symbol at a sun-watching site marked as sacred.

A fourth pictograph, a sun symbol, was found nearby and establishes that the spot was a place where the rising sun lined up with geologic features on the horizon. If Chacoan sun priests were observing the sky from this point during the summer of 1054, they could very well have seen the supernova.

Skeptics say this star and moon pictograph bears a strong resemblance to a similar one in a sun shrine on the Zuni Reservation. It is commonly agreed that the Zuni "star" represents the planet Venus. Whether the Anasazi actually observed and recorded the birth of a supernova cannot be determined. But if they did, their skills in astronomical observation were on a par with the advanced civilizations in China and other parts of the world.

More than 150 years of meticulous archaeological examination have forced the silent ruins of Chaco Canyon to give up some of their secrets, but often a new discovery simply emphasizes how little we know, or will ever know, about these remarkable people. A good example is the enigma of Chaco's stone circles.

Scattered around the ruins are 20 large circular areas outlined by low masonry walls. In most cases, the walls have disintegrated with time, leaving only the larger stones and a scattering of smaller ones. The walls appear to have served only as delineations of each circle, or perhaps they may have been low windbreaks.

Within each circled area, small, shallow stone basins were carved into the bedrock. The basins seem to make no sense to modern observers; they served no discernible practical purpose. We have no evidence they were used for grinding corn, nor had they been used as hearths. The basins vary significantly in circumference and depth, so they could not have been useful as pot-rests. There is no evidence that roofs were ever built over the circles, so it is not likely that the basins served to secure roof supports. Rock art found in the vicinity of these strange formations has offered no helpful clues.

It was not until 1974 that the Anasazi circles were given systematic study. Thomes C. Windes, of the National Park Service's Chaco Resource Division, produced detailed mapping of the stone circles, and began to wonder whether they were part of an astronomical scheme of alignments. When he had mapped lines between all the basins, the result was a bewildering maze of lines, running in all directions.

Cautiously, Windes eventually theorized that the circles might be shrines used for dances or dance-staging areas. The basins seem to have been positioned as water catchments, he thought, and therefore might have been symbolic representations of *sipapus*, or sacred springs.

His detailed research may, or may not, have solved the mystery of the circles and basins. His theory, unfortunately, rests on the following hoary, if wholly inadequate, archaeologists' axiom: "If it can't be explained, it must be ceremonial".

One of the most perplexing of Chaco Canyon's mysteries is the puzzle of Anasazi burial customs.

Research has proven that the Ancient Ones inhabited this canyon for at least 300 years. During that time, tens of thousands of people lived out their lives in the great pueblos. Yet only a few skeletal remains have been found during the century and a half of very thorough excavation. No large burial sites were discovered, and precious few individual graves were found. What, then, did the Anasazi do with their dead?

The skeletons that have been discovered suggest that the Anasazi had no special burial customs. "We are thoroughly mystified," wrote a pioneering Chaco archaeologist, Edgar L. Hewett, in 1936. "The dead were buried in very casual and miscellaneous ways, as in refuse heaps, under brick debris, occasionally in house rooms, a few in small burial mounds, usually quite near the surface. The only sign of mortuary tradition is that pottery and a few other artifacts were usually buried with the dead, but this was not an inflexible custom."

Why was it that a few people were buried within or near the pueblos, while countless others were not? How were such choices made? The almost random, disorganized procedures for burial seem totally incongruent with what must have been a highly-organized society.

Many theories have arisen about the Anasazi dead; one by one, the theories have been discarded. The first possibility seemed a logical one. The deceased had been taken to special sites, sacred places beyond the developed areas. However, in spite of years of careful research, not one such place has been located.

Cremation was ruled out early on. No burned areas or calcined bone fragments could be found. The ashes of all of Chaco's firepits and stone fireboxes were sifted and re-sifted without discovery of a single bit of human bone.

In desperation, Neil Judd, who had searched diligently for missing cemeteries, finally suggested in jest that the dead must have been placed on rafts and floated "down the Chaco (arroyo) and into the San Juan, thence into the Colorado and the Gulf of California." He concluded, "The alluvial fan at the mouth of the Rio Colorado is certainly one place I never thought to look for Chacoan burials."

Without doubt, many of the easily accessible burials were destroyed by early grave-robbing pothunters who descended upon Chaco Canyon like vultures. Even after estimates of the probable number of skeletons lost in unauthorized excavations is factored in, those can account for only about five percent of the presumed Anasazi dead.

Perhaps even more fascinating is the mystery of the Chacoan road system. A people who traveled only on foot built a far-flung system of engineered, standardized roadways.

Europeans' first awareness of the Chacoan road network came in 1879, when an Army survey expedition reported finding remarkable trails running from pueblo to pueblo "without swerving to the right or left, over valley, plain or ascent of mesas—as though the trail was older than the mesas."

It was not until a century later, in the 1970s, that the full extent of the road system became recognized. Aerial photographs taken when the sun angle was low and casting shadows revealed ancient roads running in perfectly straight lines to the north, south and southwest from Chaco Canyon's ruins. The roads crossed hills and mesas without detouring around them, were carefully cleared of all rock and were uniformly 30 feet wide.

Why such width and linear perfection? Why didn't the Anasazi choose the paths of least resistance and follow the terrain contours, as all other North American Indian paths do? Why were their roads nearly as wide as modern residential streets?

The Ancient Ones' road system extended for hundreds of miles, distinctly unlike the short, perfunctory ceremonial avenues that lead up to prehistoric settlements in other parts of the world. Segments of the Chacoan roads have since been discovered far beyond the borders of the Chacoan region, extending on into Colorado and Arizona.

What purpose could such carefully engineered and constructed roads have served for a people with no carts, no wagons, and no pack animals?

It can be surmised, of course, that the roads served a ceremonial purpose. The roads linking Chaco Canyon to outlying Anasazi pueblos are thought to have been used to transport food. Much of the canyon's population had to be supplied with foods—game, meat, berries, piñón nuts and other commodities—from other parts of their domain. Conversely, the Anasazi of the canyon could have traded off surplus corn and beans for imported items.

Almost as surely, the sophisticated roads were used as logging roads. One can imagine long processions of laborers bearing logs and firewood to met the needs of the city dwellers. There is considerable evidence that Indian traders from Mexico's advanced cultures also visited Chaco Canyon regularly, where they exchanged turquoise for macaws, conch shell trumpets and tiny copper bells.

With their imposing constructions of towns and roads, the Anasazi accomplished more than any other North Americans of their time. Yet strangely they abandoned it all. That is the final mystery of the Anasazi: why did they leave their magnificent pueblos, and where did they go?

Scholars have determined that their exodus began in the last half of the 13th Century. The abandonment was gradual; there is reason to believe the people intended to return. In many cases, the buildings' exterior openings had been walled up to protect the interiors from weather and intruders; jewelry was sometimes hidden under sand and ashes in the floors of the rooms.

Tree ring dating shows that this period of the 13th Century was one of prolonged drought. But it is clear that the Anasazi had survived previous droughts of equal severity, teaching them to stockpile food for the hard times. Therefore, we must assume that there was a combination of causes for the desertion of the Chacoan pueblos and the end of their magnificent civilization.

The peaceful Anasazi were periodically raided by fierce, nomadic tribes from the north. While the Anasazi were unassailable behind their stone walls, they could not protect their fields and crops from marauders. Perhaps, as the drought reduced their crops and their enemies plundered much of what little they were able to raise, the Anasazi had no choice but to begin drifting away. Since they apparently left at different times and in small groups, they may have become too scattered to reorganize and return.

The question of where the Anasazi went has been an easier mystery to solve. The Hopis of Arizona and the Zunis of New Mexico are sure the Chacoan peoples are among their ancestors. Traditions among the Hopi and Zuni do bear unmistakable similarities to those of the Chacoan people. And once the link between the Chacoan Anasazi and the Hopis and Zunis is conceded, there is little doubt that part of the Chacoan exodus also led to the pueblos along the Rio Grande.

The displaced master-builders of Chaco Canyon did not simply fade away. They went on to build elsewhere, passing their wisdom on to others, planting the original seeds that grew into the beautiful, enduring culture of New Mexico's Pueblo Indians.

HOW TO GET TO CHACO CANYON

Fifty-nine miles northwest of Cuba, New Mexico, on State Road 44 is Blanco Trading Post. Take State Road 56 south for 26 miles to Chaco Culture National Historic Park. The first ruin encountered is Casa Chiquita. Continuing down the road toward the Park Visitor's Center, you will pass Kin Kletso, Pueblo del Arroyo, Pueblo Bonito, Chetro Ketl, Hungo Pavi, Kin Nahasbas and Una Vida. These were all separate communities within the canyon.

Fajada Butte can be seen to the southwest of the Visitor's Center. The Sun Dagger is near the top of the imposing butte, but special permission is now required to climb it. Gallo Campground is 1.5 miles east of the Visitor's Center.

An extremely rewarding scenic sidetrip is a hike through the Ah-shi-sle-pah Badlands, located along the west side of State Road 56, just north of the park boundary. Ask at the Visitor's Center for specific directions to the trailhead.

A relatively accessible site for viewing a segment of the mystifying Chacoan road system is found by another sidetrip, to Pueblo Pintado. Leaving Chaco Canyon headed south, turn east on State Road 197 to arrive at the small Bureau of Indian Affairs town of Pueblo Pintado. The town is named for the imposing Anasazi ruins seen on the horizon to the west. Just west of the main, paved entrance to the town is a dirt road that meanders northwesterly toward the ruin.

Entrance to the ruins is on the west side, facing Chaco Canyon about 15 miles away. The Chacoan road that links Pueblo Pintado to the canyon can still be seen today as a slight, nearly imperceptible swale, or linear depression, in the terrain. Long since filled with blown sand, the road segment here can best be seen about 50 yards west of the ruins.

BIBLIOGRAPHY

MYSTERIES OF THE ANASAZI
Chapter Twelve

Brugge, David M. **A History of the Chaco Navajos.** Albuquerque. National Park Service, Division of Chaco Research. U.S. Department of the Interior. 1980.

Claiborne, Robert. **The First Americans.** New York. Time-Life Books. 1973.

Frazier, Kendrick. **People of Chaco: A Canyon and its Culture.** New York. W.W. Norton & Company. 1986.

Gladwin, Harold Sterling. **The Chaco Branch Excavations at White Mound & in the Red Mesa Valley.** Globe, Arizona. Medallion Papers. 1945.

Hewett, Edgar L. **Handbooks of Archaeological History.** Albuquerque. University of New Mexico Press. 1936.

Judge, James and Schelber, John D. **Recent Research on Chaco Prehistory.** Albuquerque. National Park Service, Division of Cultural Research, U.S. Department of the Interior. 1984.

Muench, David and Pike, Donald G. **Anasazi: Ancient People of the Rock.** Palo Alto, California. American West Publishing Company. 1974.

Windes, Thomas C. **Stone Circles of Chaco Canyon, Northwestern New Mexico.** National Park Service, Division of Chaco Research, U.S. Department of the Interior. 1978.

13

LOZEN, WOMAN WARRIOR WITH MAGIC POWERS

The Great River was flooded. Churning brown waters swirled wildly in their mad rush to Mexico. Nervous Indians rode up and down the banks looking for a safe place to cross, but there was none.

It was 1875, and the Warm Springs Apaches were on the run again. They had been ordered to leave their reservation at Ojo Caliente, in New Mexico's San Mateo Mountains. They were to be force-marched to the burnt-out wastelands of the San Carlos Reservation in

Arizona. Instead, they rebelled, fleeing south to Cuchillo Canyon, then east to the Rio Grande.

Their escape was cut short by the swollen river. Apache women sang a prayer to the River God, but the water seemed only to rise higher. They threw pieces of turquoise into the roiling waters, but still the River God would not be appeased. Time was growing short. The warriors had stayed behind, fighting desperately to delay the pursuing Blue Coats. Clearly the escaping women, children and elderly would have to keep moving; they would have to cross soon.

"Is there no one here to lead us?" cried an ancient shaman.

Then, from the center of the milling throng, came a commotion. The crowd parted and a single rider clopped to the front—a stunning woman on a coal black horse. With her long, raven hair flowing behind her, a rifle raised high above her head, she guided her horse right to the water's edge. Disturbed by the torrent, the horse balked. But the woman kicked its flanks and the horse plunged in to begin the swim.

Now the others followed. Soon the muddy Rio Grande was filled with struggling ponies and awkward swimmers. A young girl screamed as her pony floundered and they were swept away. Instantly, the Apache band's new leader splashed to the girl's side to grab the reins of the frightened mount. Stumbling and dunking, she led the terrified youngster to the opposite bank. Eventually everyone was safely across.

Still, they were hardly safe.

The strong-faced Apache woman who had taken charge now pointed to the San Andrés Mountains on the eastern horizon. "Go there," she told the others. "Camp at the hidden spring and wait. I will be there later. Now, I must go back and join the warriors."

With that, she turned her horse back across the raging river once more and galloped off to the west.

That woman's name was Lozen. Although she is all but completely forgotten today, she was once a living legend among her own people. History accords her only scattered references, since her remarkable deeds have been overshadowed by the feats of male warriors of her time. Yet Lozen rode across the landscape of New Mexico's history as dramatically as any man. Throughout all the tragic Apache wars and the long captivity that followed, she was always there, fighting along side the men and caring for the sick and wounded. It seems unfitting that Lozen has been denied a major pedestal in history, while dubious heroes like Kit Carson and Billy the Kid have become unforgettable additions to our folklore.

Research has turned up only one photograph taken of Lozen; it is now in the archives of the Bureau of American Ethnology. She is sitting beside a train, a prisoner like the rest of her tribe. A strand of hair has fallen across her proud face, but her eyes are defiant and undefeated.

Southwestern Historian Eve Ball mentioned Lozen often in her epic book *In the Days of Victorio*. James Kawaykla, a Warm Springs Apache who lived to the age of 90 at Fort Sill, Oklahoma, remembered her well, and a few other historians have acknowledged her important role in the Apache's struggle. From these meager sources, it is possible to piece together her extraordinary story.

Lozen was the sister of the great war chief, Victorio, surely one of the most heroic, misunderstood and tragic figures in the history of the West. His life's goal was the salvation of the Apache people, to keep them free, to keep them alive. Therefore, his life was one of war. Throughout most of Victorio's battles, his sister, Lozen, was by his side.

For her dedication and leadership, Lozen was respected, even revered by her people. Her wisdom and courage earned her an honored place in the circle around the council fires of the men. Her strange, mystical powers were greatly valued by all in her tribe. She was not only a warrior, she was also a *di-yin*, a medicine woman of the most holy stature.

When she was young, Lozen was strikingly beautiful. It was said that no man who saw her ever forgot her face. Though she was courted by many men, she refused them all, remaining single, chaste and holy. There is an interesting story, told to Eve Ball by James Kawaykla, which at least partially explains why Lozen chose not to marry. The story was told to Kawaykla by his Apache grandmother.

The old woman said that one day, when Lozen was quite young, Apache sentinels perched on the ridges above their stronghold sighted a lone horseman galloping toward their mountain hideout from the east. Hot on his heels came a full troop of U.S. Cavalry. The rider entered the foothills and began climbing the upper slopes. When he came within shouting distance, the Apaches called out to him, gesturing at a hiding place nearby. He found the spot, and concealed himself and his horse from the Blue Coats who passed on by.

After the danger had passed, the rider emerged to greet the Apaches who had aided him. He was a young Indian, tall, very powerful and extremely handsome, the story said. But the language he spoke was one the Apaches had never heard. He went with them to their camp and remained for some time. The stranger began to learn a little of the Apache tongue so that he could eventually tell his benefactors a little about himself and his past.

His name, he said, was Grey Ghost. He was a chieftain in a tribe that lived far toward the rising sun. That was all the Apaches ever learned about the strange young man. They never knew why he had fled to their territory, nor where he went when he left them. Throughout his stay with the Apache band, Lozen watched him constantly. She never spoke to him, and he never addressed her; he apparently departed not knowing that he would remain forever fixed in her memory and in her heart. From the day of his depar-

LOZEN. Shown in this 1886 photograph, second from the right in front of a train that would take her tribe into a Florida exile, the Apache's mystic woman warrior remained defiant.

Bureau of American Ethnology

ture, it was said, Lozen showed no interest in any other man.

Instead, she began her initiation into the mystic realm of the Apache's healing arts. Through prayer and self-sacrifice, tests of hunger and courage, she became a medicine woman with exceptional powers and skills.

She was capable of far more, in fact. Employing her skills, meditation and intuition, she also became one of the Apaches' greatest warriors. Women warriors were rare among the Apache, but not completely unheard of. John Cremony, one of the best authorities on the 19th Century Apaches, admitted he had met only one. Her name, he said, was Dexterous Horsethief, a moniker that spoke for itself.

Although Apache women were seldom warriors, they were always expected to fight in emergencies. The Apache culture was laced with war. Had it not been so, in all probability they would not have survived, would not have earned the honor of being the last American Indians to lay down their arms in front of the invading white man.

Despite the women's willingness to engage in battle, several tribal taboos prevented all but a special few from riding the warpath with the men. Among Apaches, it was widely believed that women walked more heavily than men. This could alert an enemy, and might influence men to walk in a heavy-footed, clumsy manner. It was also believed that if a menstruating woman stepped over a man's rifle, the weapon would never shoot straight again. And worse yet, if a woman poked a fire with the wrong end of a stick, she could cause bad luck for an entire warparty. To the Apache men, it was fairly obvious that a woman's place was in the wiki-up; her best role was to sing prayers while the warriors were away.

But that was not Lozen's role.

Lozen's lifespan coincided with severely troubled times in the Apache nation. They were beseiged from all sides. The Apache's endless war with Mexico dragged on and on; daily more white men and more troops moved onto their lands. The Apaches' resistence was always strong, but one by one, their warriors fell. Their leaders recognized they had only two choices: reservation life or extermination. For a time, it seemed they had deliberately chosen the latter.

In 1879, Victorio made his famous vow "to make war forever" against the white man. "I prefer to die in my own land," he said. "I will leave my bones among the bones of my people."

Victorio led his people on an epic migration, out of New Mexico into Texas, then back to the Sacramento Range, through Dog Canyon, across the Tularosa Basin, and on to Mexico—and Tres Castillos.

East of the Sacramentos, Lozen stayed behind to aid an expectant mother who could no longer travel. She and the young woman hid in a thicket as the others rode on. Had Lozen remained with the warriors, the terrible ambush at Tres Castillos might never have taken place.

Her magical powers, her perceptions, had saved the Apaches more than once by that time. Whenever the band camped for the night, Lozen would go immediately to the nearest hilltop to stand, arms outstretched, palms raised and cupped, her face upturned to the sky. She would enter a trance and sing to the Apache god, Ussen, as she slowly revolved to face each of the four directions in turn. If there were enemies anywhere nearby, her palms would begin to tingle; it was said by those who watched her that her hands turned a deep purple when she faced the direction of enemies. By the intensity of the tingling, she could determine their proximity.

If she sensed no danger, she would return to camp and report "No enemy is near", assuring all they could bed down for the night.

But the Apaches had no such warning when they entered the rocky hills of Tres Castillos on October 13, 1880.

As the name implies, Tres Castillos is a location where three castle formations of jagged rock rise up from the desolate Sonoran desert floor, north and slightly east of Chihuahua. The Apaches often stopped there to water and graze their horses. This time, there were also Mexican soldiers, ready and waiting.

The ambush took the weary Indians completely by surprise. The Mexican commander, Joaquín Terrazas, used an Indian tactic with deadly effectiveness. He marched a small detachment of his men forward to meet the encamping Apaches. Thinking they faced only 20 men, the Apache warriors mounted up and charged—directly into the main Mexican force 219 strong and well-armed.

The Apaches fell back to Cerro del Sur, the southernmost of the rocky knolls, but the Mexicans quickly surrounded them. The fighting went on throughout the night, but by 10:00 a.m. the following morning, it was all over. Victorio was dead, along with 77 of his people. Joaquín Terrazas collected $17,250 in bounty money for their scalps.

Survivors of the Tres Castillos massacre regrouped in the Escaramuza Mountains to the south, having crept there on their hands and knees during the night. The old War Chief Nana and his forces found them a few days later. Aged through he was, Nana shouldered the burden left him by Victorio, taking command of the remaining Apache warriors. With the aid of Mangas and Kaytennae, he led his stunned but stoic band back to Arizona.

Lozen had not been seen for several weeks. It was assumed that she, like her brother, was dead. Nana kept his people constantly on the move, from the Mogollón Mountains to Ojo Caliente, from there to Cook's Pass and back once again to the *barrancas* of Mexico. Even if Lozen still lived, there was almost no way she would ever find her wandering people.

Sure enough, one day in the spring of 1881, the Apache sentinels spotted a lone rider approaching their stronghold. The rider carried a rifle, led a pack horse and stayed bent in the saddle, looking down to read signs in the sand.

When the rider came close enough, the hiding Apaches could tell it was a woman. Expectantly, Nana rode out to greet her, raising his rifle above his head in a salute reserved for male warriors. It was Lozen all right, and she had accomplished the impossible, tracking down her people after months of wandering.

That night, around the ceremonial fires, she was asked to tell the story of her long separation from her people. Lozen recalled that she had taken the pregnant young woman to a hiding place on the banks of the Rio Grande, where she attended the birth of a new member of the Apache tribe. Having wrapped the baby in a fragment of blanket, she left the new mother to search for food.

Near the river, she saw a herd of longhorn steers. With a knife, she attacked and killed one of those great beasts . . . a feat few men would have attempted. Next she carved a bridle from the steer's hide and made a tsach-cradle using willow shoots. That night, she swam the river and entered Mexico.

A troop of Mexican cavalry was camped not far away; a single sentry paced back and forth in front of the hobbled horses. Lozen crept in close and when the guard went to the fire to warm himself, she slipped like a shadow among the horses. She tied her handmade bridle around the jaws of a horse, slashed the hobbles with her knife, and rode out through the center of the camp. The startled soldiers sprang up from their serapes. Spanish curses filled the air as Lozen drove her frenzied mount over the bank and into the river. There was a roar of rifles behind her and bullets skipped off the water as she made her escape.

When she reached the opposite shore, the waiting Apache mother swung onto the horse with the cradled baby on her back.

Day after day, they traveled east, with Lozen walking most of the time. Their only food was the dried beef from the poached longhorn, their only moisture was the crushed pulp of the prickly pear. Finally they came to a Mexican line camp, where a few *vaqueros* had quartered their horses in a thornbush corral.

Lozen left the young mother with the horse and instructed her to be ready to ride at dawn. Then the Apache warrior woman slipped away into the darkness.

Next morning as the sun peeked over the hills, one of the cowboys walked out to the corral and swung open the gate. Instantly, a horse and rider flashed by him and were gone before he could open his mouth.

Now that both Lozen and the young mother had horses, they could travel much faster. Lozen managed to kill a straggling American Blue Coat, from whom she stole a rifle, saddle, shirt and canteen—all of which made travel much easier. Not long after that, they reached the Mescalero Apache band in the Sacramento Mountains above Dog Canyon. There Lozen learned about the tragedy of Tres Castillos and the death of her brother.

Her grief was overpowering, but the Mescaleros tried to console her. "The past cannot be changed," they said. "Stay here with us. Here, at least, you will be safe."

Lozen only shook her head. The next morning she rode away, leaving the mother and baby with the Mescaleros. It took her weeks to find Nana and the Warm Springs Apaches, but when she did, she immediately took her rightful place among the remaining warriors of her brother's band.

Apache War Chief Nana was, in fact, a brilliant tactician. For months, he won all his battles and stole hundreds of horses. But even though Nachez, Loco, Chato and Geronimo all eventually joined him, the tide inevitably turned. The Apaches found themselves harder pressed than ever.

In 1883, two Apache women—Lozen and Dahteste—were sent to arrange a meeting with Lieutenant Britton Davis. In the peace conference that followed, Davis offered the Apaches a reservation on Turkey Creek in Arizona. The Indians accepted, and for two years, there was an uneasy peace throughout the Apache nation. Conditions were harsh on the reservation and, as always, the treaty promises were quickly broken. The cattle that had been promised never arrived; a once-proud people now stood in line for skimpy rations and handouts from their conquerors.

It was a situation that could not last very long.

In the spring of 1885, the desert wind wafted gently through the Apache reservation, bringing with it the delicate scent of the flowering palo verdes and greasewood blossoms. On the hills above, the haughty saguaros bloomed white over the bright yellow prickly pear flowers that sprawled across the rocks.

In the White Mountains of the Arizona Territory, it was *T'aa'nacho*, the Season of Many Leaves. On the white man's calendar, it was May 17.

Geronimo sat in the doorway of his wiki-up, silently gazing at his village. His snapping-turtle mouth was drawn tightly shut and his deep, black eyes were narrow slits in his wrinkled face. He had been drinking all day, but the alcohol seemed to have had no effect. He was quiet, sullen, brooding.

Behind him, Mangas, Nachez, Chihuahua and the aged Nana sat on the earthen floor of the hut and stared impassively at the stony-faced Apache leader. They, too, had been drinking and yet they also were silent. They waited for Geronimo to speak.

At last he said, "We have tried to live by their rules. We have given up the warpath and become farmers. We have tried to live on his reservation, and it is the life of a dog. An Apache's feet were not meant to follow a plow and our war ponies were not meant to pull them."

Geronimo's leathery face twisted into a mask of pent-up anger. "We could fight them here," he said. "We could fight and die, here on this ground."

Nana shook his wise old head. "It would serve no purpose. Too many others would die with us. The time has come to leave this place. All of us."

Geronimo turned his face to the wind. There was a smell of freedom in the spring air, and he breathed it deeply. *"Enjah!"* he said. "Good! Let us go tonight. Let us ride to the mountains of Mexico, where we can live like Apaches instead of dogs."

That night, over 100 Apache men, women and children slipped away from their reservation. They quietly bundled their possessions, saddled their ponies and vanished. As they rode beneath the telegraph lines, Geronimo stood up in his stirrups. His knife flashed and the wires fell to the ground. The last Apache war had begun.

There were only 38 warriors in Geronimo's band when the Apaches made their final bid for freedom—38 fighters facing almost insurmountable odds. Yet this handful of Indians would, for the next 16 months, terrify the Southwest and defy the combined armies of the United States and Mexico.

Thirty-seven of these warriors were men: the other was Lozen.

Once the reservation boundaries were behind them, Geronimo split his forces into small groups. The Apaches fled in many directions, knowing that all trails could not be followed. Chihuahua was the unlucky leader. He and his band ran north along the Mogollón Rim. They were the first to be found. Lieutenant Davis' troops attacked their camp atop a cliff near the Verde River. There, many of Chihuahua's people were killed or captured before the rest broke out of the trap and fought on into Mexico.

Days later, as the Apaches regrouped in the Sierra Madre, a massive military campaign was launched against them. Eighty companies of U.S. Cavalry, led by

Indian scouts, thundered across the border in search of the Apaches, while hundreds of Mexican soldiers, led by Tarahumara scouts, took to the field as well. The odds were overwhelming. The best the Apaches could do was to keep on the move. Fight and run, and run again. Month after desperate month, they crossed and re-crossed the Sierra Madre.

Every night before camping, Lozen would climb to the highest point and sing to Ussen. When she had determined the nearness of the enemy, other warriors would slip off into the twilight to build a false camp far away—a circle of campfires that would lure the pursuers in the wrong direction. Had it not been for Lozen's magical powers, the Geronimo campaign might not have lasted as long as it did.

By July 1886, Geronimo knew he could not win. He gave up fighting and sought only to hide. Even that was not possible. Finally, once again, Lozen and Dahteste were sent to open peace negotiations with the Americans. While the two Apache women were in the American camp, a violent incident occurred.

Lozen had come in under a flag of truce, riding directly into the enemy camp. While she may have needed Ussen's powers to find the encampment, and though she knew her personal safety was tenuous even during a truce, she surely had no reason to believe the camp itself would be attacked. Perhaps when she stood among the American soliders, her palms tingled no matter what direction she faced.

In any event, a company of Mexican *Rurales* suddenly stumbled onto the cavalry camp. Seeing the Apache women, the Mexicans misunderstood the situation and opened fire. Neither Lozen nor Dahteste was hit, but the valiant American captain, Emmett S. Crawford, was fatally shot when he sprang atop a boulder to wave his white undershirt in an attempt to stop the shooting.

Following Crawford's death, Lieutenant Maus made the initial contact with Geronimo. Shortly thereafter, Lieutenant Charles B. Gatewood sat down beside the aged Indian chief in the hot, mottled shade of a thorny ravine to work out terms for a surrender.

The conditions laid down by the Americans were severe. The Apaches were to be removed to Florida, far from their desert homelands. Reluctantly, Geronimo accepted. He and his people were shipped by train to an alien, tropical world. The wars had ended but the struggle to survive went on.

Florida's humid heat took its toll on the desert people. Many of them died, but Lozen's knowledge of herbal medicines saved countless others. In 1887, the Apaches were sent to Alabama. It was there that Lozen died.

According to Elbys Hugar, curator of the Mescalero Apache Cultural Center, Lozen was buried at either Mount Vernon or Fort Marion, Alabama.

Lozen's gravemarker probably bore no special epitaph, but if it had, the words of her brother, Victorio, might have suited it best: "Lozen is as my right hand. Strong as a man, braver than most, and cunning in strategy—Lozen is a shield to her people."

BIBLIOGRAPHY

LOZEN: WOMAN WARRIOR WITH MAGIC POWERS
Chapter Thirteen

Adams, Alexander B. **Geronimo.** New York. Berkley Medallion Books. 1971.

Ball, Eve. **In the Days of Victorio.** Tucson, Ariz. University of Arizona Press. 1970.

Bigelow, Lt.John. **On the Bloody Trail of Geronimo.** New York. Tower Publication. 1968.

Brown, Dee. **Bury My Heart at Wounded Knee.** New York. Holt, Rinehart and Winston. 1970.

Cremony, John. **Life Among the Apaches.** Alexandria, Va. Time-Life Books. (Reprint) 1980.

Opler, Morris. **An Apache Lifeway.** New York. American Folklore Society. 1938.

Thrapp, Dann. **Victorio and the Mimbres Apaches.** Tucson, Ariz. University of Arizona Press. 1968.

14

THE STORY OF THE APACHE KID

South of Socorro, on the eastern edge of the San Augustín Plains, stands a dark, brooding range of mountains—tall, wild and forbidding. From a distance these mountains resemble a reclining body, a corpse laid to rest on the desert floor. Vick's Peak is the skull and the ridge that wanders to the north forms the rest of the body blanketed in ponderosa pines.

Today we call these the San Mateo Mountains. A hundred years ago, they were known as *Dzil-shis-inday*. In the 19th Century, this range was one of the Apache leader Victorio's favorite places of refuge.

From the summit of the San Mateos, the twisting Rio Grande is visible, shimmering in the east, while off to the west, the landscape dissolves into a pastel mirage, blue and pink and endless. The lower slopes of the San Mateos are hot and dry, fragrant with piñón and juniper. But up on the ridge crests, up where the wind blows, it is fresh and cool.

It was along this crest line, in September 1909, that a posse of nine deputized Black Range ranchers tracked the last, great Apache outlaw, The Apache Kid, to the foot of the peak that now bears his name. It was there, high in the golden aspens, that the final act in a long and tragic drama was played out.

The beginnings of The Apache Kid's story are lost. In fact, historians are uncertain of his real name. Most have said he was first called *Ski-be-nan-ted*. Others contend the name was *Oska-ben-nan-telz*, which translates as "Terrible Tempered". Other references say his translated name was "Four Fingers", or "Crazy One", or "Hears Something in the Night". Perhaps the strangest name attributed to The Apache Kid was *Haskay-bay-nay-nytl*, meaning, "Tall, brave man destined to come to a mysterious end".

He may have been a White Mountain Apache, but more likely he was a full-blooded Coyotero. He is believed to have been born in the 1860s near Globe, Arizona, eldest of seven children and grandson of a minor chief, Toggedechuse. When he was very young, he and his mother were captured by the Yumas. These latter raised him until he was recaptured during one of General George A. Crook's Arizona campaigns.

He was about 12 years old at that time, wise beyond his years and very adaptable. Back at Globe, he earned his livelihood cleaning the saloons and running errands for shopkeepers in the booming frontier town. It was a poor life for any child, and infinitely worse for a little Apache boy adrift in the white man's world. The youngster was living a hand-to-mouth existence, surviving by his wits, when he was discovered by Al Sieber, chief of scouts for the United States Army, Department of Arizona.

Albert Sieber was already a legend in his own time. A veteran of Gettysburg who went west after the Civil War, he soon gained renown as an Indian fighter. In 1871, he signed up as a scout for General Crook, and went to war against the Apaches for nearly two decades. He was, as General Nelson Miles once said, "the most self-contained and most fearless scout in the service."

Sieber's ability to command the Indians serving under him stemmed primarily from mutual respect. "Sieber's Scouts" were willing to die for him, and often did, because he never lied to them, was always fair, and most importantly, because he understood them. Perhaps, it was his insight into the special nature of the 19th Century Apaches that caused him to befriend this particular Apache urchin in Globe.

Sieber took the youngster under his wing, got him out of the barrooms and alleys and gave him a new home: "Hell's Forty Acres", as the U.S. Army Post at San Carlos was known. The Apache youth was employed as an orderly of sorts, and a messenger boy for the garrison. Sieber taught him the English language and showed him how to cook the white man's food. The benefactor also gave the boy a new name: "Kid".

For a while at least, the Indian boy and the white scout were very much like father and son. They were inseparable. As soon as The Kid was old enough, he enlisted in the Army scouts as well. He rose quickly to the rank of sergeant and, within two years, made first sergeant. During the Geronimo campaigns, 1885-86, The Kid rode at Sieber's side.

In spite of all that followed, his reputation as a scout has never been impugned. The Apache Kid was one of the best.

As a grown man, he stood five-foot-nine and weighed a trim 150 pounds. His handsome features and cat-like grace made him extremely popular among the young Apache women near San Carlos. He was an excellent shot and his eyesight was said to be nothing short of phenomenal.

He transacted an influential marriage, wedding one of Chief Eskiminzin's daughters. His wife's Apache name, like his own, is lost to history. At San Carlos, she was known as "The Beauty."

The Apache Kid was headed for a career of distinguished service, achieving an honored position in an alien army. His future looked much brighter than that of most Indians living on the poverty-stricken reservation. Then, fate intervened and changed his life and the course of history.

One night, The Kid's grandfather, old Toggedechuse, invited some of his friends to join him in drinking *tiswin*, a home-brewed beer made of sprouted corn. The get-together, as all too often happened, turned into a free-for-all drunken brawl. It ended in gunplay and the death of Toggedechuse. All present agreed the fatal shot into Toggedechuse's back came from the chief's long-time rival and blood enemy, an Apache named "Rip".

The Apache Kid grieved at his grandfather's death, but his training in the white man's military discipline was strong enough to restrain him from seeking revenge. He brooded but did nothing.

Several months later, in the summer of 1887, Sieber and Captain Pierce left for an inspection tour of the White River Subagency. In their absence, Sergeant Kid was placed in charge of the scouts, and was made acting chief of the tribal police.

A few days after Pierce and Sieber departed, word came to the post that a big drinking party was in progress in the shady ceremonial grove along the river. With the white chiefs gone, the rougher elements among the clans thought it a good opportunity to throw a party. In addition to feasting, dancing and gambling, there was fighting and brawling. More celebrants were arriving by the hour.

Lieutenant F. B. Fowler, in command during Captain Pierce's absence, sent The Kid and a few scouts to break up the drunken party before someone got killed.

As The Kid and his men approached, smoke from the cooking fires drifted up through the cottonwoods. The Kid read his orders aloud, but was greeted by jeers and hooting. "Let us alone, Kid!" they shouted. "Go back to your white friends. This is an Indian party."

Someone else shouted, "You're an Indian, too, Kid . . . or have you forgotten? Come. Have a drink with your brothers!"

The Kid hesitated, torn by loyalty to the white man's Army and love for his own people. Someone handed him a bottle of whiskey. The rhythm of the dancing throbbed in his head. He dropped lightly down from his horse and tilted up the bottle. By late afternoon, The Kid and his fellow scouts were as drunk as the rest. Just before sundown, another band of Apaches rode into the grove and joined the festivities. At their head rode the outlaw Rip.

With his emotions inflamed by the whiskey, The Kid went for his gun and shot Rip dead.

When Al Sieber returned from White River a few days later, he found The Kid and four scouts still absent from duty. Angry and disappointed by his protege's behavior, Sieber was sulking in his tent when a sentry reported a row of Indians coming toward the post on horseback, single file. Five very hung over Apaches stopped at the edge of the garrison and dismounted as Sieber walked out to meet them. He stared sullenly at The Kid, then motioned for him to follow. As they walked toward Sieber's tent, a crowd of curious Apache onlookers fell in behind them. At the tent, Captain Pierce demanded the five AWOL scouts turn in their rifles, sidearms and cartridges. This they did, hanging them over a caneback chair near the tent.

"You have been absent five days without permission," Captain Pierce intoned. "I order you to the calaboose."

Antonio Diaz, a Mexican translator, interpreted the command which was met with stony silence. "Calaboose," Diaz repeated.

The Kid glanced at this friends. They had expected this. They had come back at The Kid's insistence; they were contrite, but they had already agreed they would not go to jail.

Then the translator made the mistake of saying he believed they would all be exiled to Florida.

Near the tent, Captain Pierce saw the crowd stirring angrily. Several Indians seated on horses brought out their rifles and cocked them.

"Look out, Sieber! They're going to fire!" the captain shouted. Immediately, a volley of shots ripped through the tent.

Sieber kicked over the chair, scattering the scout's firearms and made a dive for his own gun. In the confusion, The Kid dashed for his horse. Sieber reappeared at the flap of the tent and fired at the mounted Indians. In an instant, he was hit; a .45-70 slug from a buffalo gun shattered his left leg just below the knee.

The Kid, still unarmed and accompanied by several others, fled the post.

Within minutes, troops were organized and took off in pursuit. After 10-15 miles the soldiers lost the Apaches as darkness fell. In the morning, additional detachments were sent out for a massive track down. After several days of searching, the renegades were cornered in the Rincón Mountains.

The Kid sent out a courier with an offer of surrender. Even now, he could not believe he was in serious trouble. Surely the Army would listen to his side of the story; they would understand that he had done nothing worse than drink forbidden whiskey with his own people, and had settled his score with Rip.

General Miles accepted the surrender offer and, true to his word, The Kid came in. At San Carlos, he listened in disbelief as he heard himself charged with shooting and maiming his best friend, Albert Sieber. A court martial was held, and The Kid, still sure he could vindicate himself, spoke in his own defense.

The court transcripts show that he ended his testimony by saying, "I think God sent a bad spirit in my heart. There are some good people and some bad people amongst them all. I am not afraid to tell all these things because I have not done very much harm. I killed only one man whose name is 'Rip', because he killed my grandfather. I am not educated like you, and therefore can't say much. If I had made any arrangements before I came in, I would not have given up my arms at Mr. Sieber's tent. That is all I have to say."

No one at the trial was able to swear they had seen The Kid shoot at anyone, or do anything except try to get away once the shooting started. Even Sieber, testifying from his hospital bed, was not sure who fired the crippling shot. The Apache Kid was shocked and disillusioned when the verdict of guilty was brought in. He and the other four mutineers were sentenced to ten years in Alcatraz. The Kid's faith in white men was destroyed forever.

While the scouts began serving their sentences, the case was reviewed by the Judge Advocate General in Washington, D.C. He determined that the military had no jurisdiction in the case since, due to an act of Congress, all Indian defendants were to be tried in civil courts. This congressional act had freed many unjustly confined Indian prisoners, but for The Kid and his companions, it simply meant a second trial, this time in territorial court.

Again, the embittered young Apache testified in his own behalf. By this time, Sieber had realized his leg would never mend properly and that he was crippled for life. He, too, now testified in bitterness, claiming The Kid was lying. The jury, all white Arizonans, accepted Sieber's new testimony, again finding the five defendants guilty. They were sentenced to seven years of hard labor in the Yuma Territorial Prison.

It was customary at that time to tattoo the foreheads of Indian convicts so they could be readily identifiable. The Kid received a "W" for warrior, an oddly prophetic mark, since he would soon become more of a warrior than he had ever been.

Arrangements were made to transport the prisoners, but Gila County Sheriff Glenn Reynolds cockily turned down a military escort. Instead he loaded his convicts into a stagecoach, and took along only an armed driver named Gene Middleton, as well as his deputy, a barroom poet known as "Hunk Dory" Holmes. A cold rain was falling as the coach rolled out of Globe on the long road to Yuma. They made 40 miles the first day and spent the night in Riverside Station.

November 2, 1889 dawned chilly and damp. The rain had stopped, but dark clouds hung in the sky; the first signs of winter were in the air. The horses strained, blowing hard as they pulled the coach through the muddy ruts. At the base of a steep hill, Reynolds ordered the prisoners out to lighten the load. The sheriff walked ahead of the heavily-manacled prisoners while his deputy followed behind, covering them with his rifle. The stage gradually pulled ahead of the walkers who trudged through the mud.

Suddenly, two of the Indians jumped Holmes and the others pounced on Reynolds.

"Hunk Dory" Holmes was the first to die. Later, it would be said he died of fright since no wounds were found on his body.

A prisoner named Pas-ten-tah grabbed Holmes' rifle and shot Sheriff Reynolds as he struggled with the Indians trying to take his shotgun. At the sound of the shot, Middleton turned in his seat on the stagecoach; he caught a bullet in the mouth, knocking him off the coach.

He lay bleeding in the mud, feigning death as the Apaches approached him. Pas-ten-tah raised the rifle to apply the coup-de-grace, but The Kid stopped him, saying in English, "The man is dead; save the cartridge."

Even in his critical condition, Middleton did not miss the significance of this remark. He realized The Kid would speak English to another Apache only if he wanted Middleton to know he was deliberately sparing his life. Mounted on stolen horses and armed with their former guards' guns, the Apaches quickly vanished into the brush. Gene Middleton staggered back down the road, seeking help.

THE APACHE KID. Some who knew him said his real name translated as "Tall, brave man destined to come to a mysterious end".

Bureau of American Ethnology

When news of the escape reached San Carlos, troops were once again dispatched to track down The Apache Kid. This time, he seemed to have disappeared without a trace. Though the search continued for weeks, no sign of him could be found. Any Apache who could be accused of aiding The Kid was sent into exile . . . to Fort Union, New Mexico, or to Florida. One of these Apaches was The Kid's father-in-law, Eskiminzin. Since his entire family was exiled with him, we can assume that The Kid's wife, "The Beauty", was among them.

In March of 1890, a Mormon freighter was ambushed and killed on the San Carlos road; his guns and goods were stolen. Next day, a troop of scouts and cavalry was sent out on the trail of the outlaws. This time the tracking team was successful. After three days of what the *Tucson Daily Citizen* would later call "the best piece of pursuit work ever accomplished in Arizona", the outlaws' camp was spotted in a boulder field high on the shoulders of the rugged Sierra Anchas range.

In the fight that followed, four of the Apache fugitives were killed; only The Kid got away.

Now he was completely on his own. With all his friends dead and no hope of finding his wife, something must have snapped in The Kid's mind. He began an unstoppable one-man reign of terror. He struck at lonely ranch houses, remote prospectors' camps and ambushed unwary travelers. He killed quickly and stole horses, guns and other goods before fading away like a phantom.

No one will ever know the extent of his depredations, for he received the blame for nearly every murder committed in the Arizona and New Mexico territories during the next four years. Many of the charges were unfounded, but enough were true to send terrified settlers packing off to the safety of the military posts.

The U.S. Army sought The Kid relentlessly. At the

height of the "Apache Kid Campaign", nearly 1,000 soldiers rode in search of the elusive outlaw. Once, while a Tenth Cavalry detachment pursued him, The Kid made a sidetrip to a nearby ranch where he shot the two ranchers, stole a fresh horse and disappeared over the border into Mexico.

In 1892, two Arizona counties, Graham and Gila, offered $500 rewards for the capture, dead or alive, of "the Indian murderer designated as The Kid". The next year, Governor Nathan O. Murphy signed into law a special bill authorizing a reward of $5,000 for The Kid. A week later, the New Mexico Legislature voted an appropriation of $2,000. The Arizona Cattleman's Association added another $2,000; Mexico's President, Porfirio Diaz, offered $5,000 more.

Fifteen thousand dollars was a lot of money for bringing down one man, so bounty hunters flocked to the hills. Still, The Apache Kid could not be found.

With the passage of time, Albert Sieber's bitterness subsided. He must have realized that unjust treatment had led his former friend to become the most wanted outlaw in the Southwest. Perhaps Sieber realized that he himself was at least partly to blame. At any rate, one day Dan Williamson, a close acquaintance of Sieber and later an Arizona historian, came to Sieber with a tale from an ex-Indian scout who claimed to know The Kid's whereabouts.

Williamson suggested they trap The Kid and collect the reward. Sieber found the idea of killing for money repugnant, but later he came up with a different idea. If the ex-scout would serve as a go-between, perhaps they could talk to The Kid and persuade him to surrender, with the understanding that the reward would all be used to procure him a pardon.

Williamson agreed it was worth a try. The two of them set up a camp in the mountains while the ex-scout went off to make the contact. Sieber and Williamson waited several nights for The Kid to show up. Williamson would later write that he was sure The Kid was often hovering nearby, watching them. But the out-law, fed up with the white man's deals, never revealed himself.

During this period, The Apache Kid frequently sought refuge in Mexico among the Yaqui Indians of the Sierra Madre. He knew he could not evade the bounty hunters forever, so with the aid of the Yaquis, he devised a plan to take the pressure off.

Late in 1894, an Apache woman walked into San Carlos to inform Captain Sedgewick Rice that she had been living with The Apache Kid in a Yaqui stronghold in Sonora. The Kid was dead now, she said, killed by a disease that sounded like tuberculosis. Her story was convincing enough that the rewards were withdrawn. It would be many years before the tale would be dis-proved.

It was in September, 15 years later, when a New Mexico cattleman, Charles Anderson, discovered two of his horses had been stolen from his ranch in the Black Range. He formed a posse of fellow ranchers and set off on the trail of the thieves. They crossed the continen-tal divide and entered the San Mateo Mountains.

Just before dark, they sighted the rustlers' camp with the stolen horses tethered nearby. The ranchers withdrew quietly into the trees for the night. An hour before dawn, they crept silently up the slope and sur-rounded the outlaws' camp. With first light, an Indian woman rose from her blankets and went to the spring for water. The cattlemen let her pass. Two Indian men got up next. As they walked toward the horses, the posse opened fire. The first shot caught the tall Indian in the throat and two more bullets shattered his chest. The woman and the other man made a dash for the woods and escaped.

While examining the dead Indian, Anderson com-mented on the odd mark on the dead man's forehead. It appeared to be a faded "W".

They left the body where it fell, took their horses and rode home. A few days later, the Indian woman made her way back to the reservation and told an incredible tale. The slain man, she said, was The Apache Kid. She had traveled with him for some time, she said, showing a large wad of money he had entrusted to her.

Upon hearing the news, Anderson shook his head and exclaimed, "Boys, we done shot us the biggest game ever killed in New Mexico!"

Anderson and some of the other ranchers went back to the scene of their ambush. Though the body was in sorry condition by this time, Anderson cut off the trigger finger as a souvenir, then decapitated the corpse. They boiled down the head and left carrying the skull as a trophy.

At this juncture in U.S. history, there was a prevalent belief that the structure of a man's skull determined his criminal propensities. Outlaw craniums were in great demand. The skull of The Apache Kid, in due time, made its way to New York where it received considerable study and comment. It yielded little of real scientific value, however, for the course of The Apache Kid's life had been shaped by factors other than the shape of his head.

Why had The Kid come back to New Mexico after all those years of hiding in Mexico? Could he have returned just to steal a few horses? Was it as simple as that, or did he come back for the huge cache of gold the Apache Chief Victorio is said to have hidden here?

According to local legends, Victorio had stashed a great treasure somewhere in New Mexico. Most of the people who searched for it believed the gold was hidden east of the Jornada del Muerto, in a long-lost cave. Others swore it was somewhere up in the San Mateos, those rugged mountains Victorio knew so well.

Could it be that The Kid knew where to find the gold? Could another outlaw, possibly a survivor of Victorio's band, have offered to show him where it was? If so, perhaps that was the real mission of The Apache Kid's last trip to the San Mateos.

If Victorio's treasure is half the size some folks say it is, the loot would have bought a lot of guns and ammunition, enough for the Apache renegades in the Sierra Madre to hold off the Mexican *Rurales* for years.

The Apache Kid had been a hunted man for nearly two decades. He had spent years on the run, constantly a step ahead of death. Surely a man who had lived as a fugitive as long as he had would develop a sixth sense about an ambush. He might have known his time was finally running out, and simply sought a good place to die.

If he wanted a place to rest his spirit, a place that would always be as wild as he was, then he chose the right spot. Even today, Apache Kid Peak is accessible only by a foot trail. The Kid's body was eventually buried amid the aspens at the site of his death. There, in this now-congressionally designated Apache Kid Wilderness Area, lies the heart of The Apache Kid.

HOW TO GET TO THE APACHE KID'S RESTING PLACE

To reach Apache Kid Peak, start at the small town of Monticello, located 25 miles northwest of Truth or Consequences. From Monticello, a graveled Forest Service Road, Number 225, goes northeast for eight miles to Springtime Campground.

From the campground, the trail The Kid once rode makes a steep two-mile ascent to the ridge of the San Mateos. Stay on this trail, Number 43, and follow the ridge north. After four miles, the path joins Trail Number 46 which branches off to the east toward Apache Kid Peak. The summit is approximately a half-mile away at that point.

There is no safe drinking water at the campground or along the trail. The visit to Apache Kid Peak is a strenuous 14-mile round trip hike.

BIBLIOGRAPHY

THE STORY OF THE APACHE KID
Chapter Fourteen

Hayes, Hess G. **Apache Vengence.** Tucson, Ariz. University of Arizona Press. 1968.

Kent, William. **Reminiscences of an Outdoor Life.** San Francisco, Calif. A.M. Robertson. 1929.

Miller, Joseph. **The Arizona Story.** New York. Hastings House. 1952.

Minutes of District Court of the Second Judicial District of the Territory of Arizona. October 25, 1889.

Ogle, Ralph. **Federal Control of Western Apaches.** Albuquerque, N.M. University of New Mexico Press. 1970.

Raine, William MacLeod. **Famous Sheriffs and Western Outlaws.** New York. New Home Library. 1944.
Thrapp, Dan. **Albert Sieber, Chief of Scouts.** Norman, Okla. University of Oklahoma Press. 1970.

15

SPACE TRAVELLERS' RENDEZVOUS

In 1947, the Land of Enchantment could easily have changed its name to the Flying Saucer Capital of America. During the summer of that year, more UFO sightings were reported in New Mexico than in any other state. Throughout June and into July, the eternally beautiful New Mexico sky was more rewarding to watch than it had ever been, both by day and by night.

The *Albuquerque Journal* gave almost daily front page accounts of the sightings. A saucer-shaped disc was seen moving south over Silver City on June 25, 1947. Two days later, a white object, glowing like a light bulb, passed over Pope, New Mexico. It showed up a short time later over White Sands Missile Range, and was last seen over San Miguél.

On the following day, an Air Force captain flying near Alamogordo watched in amazement as a ball of fire, trailing a blue flame, streaked beneath his aircraft.

On June 29, an aerial object was reported to have fallen near Cliff, New Mexico. Army Air Force personnel searched the area but found nothing other than a peculiar smell in the air. Later that same day, a team of naval rocket test experts watched a silver-colored disc perform intricate aerial maneuvers high above the White Sands test range. Next morning, a Tucumcari woman stood on her front porch, watching a yellowish, circular object as it traveled from east to west at an incredible speed across the lower part of the sky. At first she thought it was a meteor, but then it slowed down and took on a circular motion as it neared the horizon.

A blue saucer was reported over Albuquerque on July 1, 1947, zig-zagging across the sky. On one wondrous occasion, a whole line of 13 silver discs flew over the city. People trooped out into their front yards, and lay on their lawns to watch as the "space ships" performed acrobatics above them.

It was one grand, unforgettable summer in New Mexico!

It was an exciting time in other ways, as well. The first atomic bomb had been created and exploded in New Mexico just two years earlier. Captured Nazi V-2 rockets were being tested at White Sands during those days also. The Space Age was dawning and the first rays of that monumental dawn were emanating from New Mexico. It seemed quite logical that if our little planet was being monitored by extra-terrestrial beings who had even the slightest interest in our rather primitive efforts, they might decide to drop by and check out what was going on in the Land of Enchantment in 1947.

It is well-known that space travel and interplanetary research have risks. Surely accidents can happen even to beings more advanced than we. Perhaps that is why, at the height of the 1947 New Mexico saucer flap, an incident occurred which received international attention... and which, to this day, causes people to wonder what *really* happened in southeastern New Mexico on the fateful night of July 2, 1947.

The drama began around 10:00 p.m. Dan Wilmot and his wife were seated on the front porch of their home in Roswell when an enormous glowing object soared over them headed northwest. The object was moving at a great rate of speed, but the Wilmots had time to dash out into their yard to observe it for 40 or 50 seconds. They described the phenomenon as oval-shaped, seemingly composed of two parts, like two inverted, linked saucers. It was glowing as if lit from within and was completely silent.

Fearing they would be ridiculed, the Wilmots did not report their experience for several days.

But that same night, a rancher named W.W. "Mac" Brazel was weathering out a storm in his small house on his sheep ranch 30 miles southeast of Corona . . . about 10 air-miles northwest of Roswell. Mac lived alone most of the time. His wife and children usually stayed in Tularosa where there was at least a school and a few amenities. Mac's little ranch had neither telephone nor radio.

On the night of July 2, two of his younger children were with him in the ranch house when an extraordinary lighting storm flashed across the land. Suddenly, in the midst of the storm, he heard an explosion—not like thunder, but something noticeably different.

The storm finally subsided and when morning came, Mac Brazel saddled up his horse and rode out to check on his sheep. As he loped across the bleak, rain-drenched pastures, he sighted a long swath of wreckage splattered out across a stretch of land on the Foster Ranch, adjacent to his own property.

Meanwhile, on that same morning, 80 to 90 air-miles to the west of the Brazel's ranch, Grady Landon "Barney" Barnett, a U.S. Soil Conservation Service engineer, was working on an assignment not far from Magdalena. He was out on the flatlands of the San Augustín Plains when he noticed sunlight reflecting off a metallic object about a mile away. His first thought was that it might be a plane crash, but when he reached the wreckage, he realized he was staring at something utterly beyond his comprehension.

The metallic object was disc-shaped, dull grey in color, and about 30 feet across. It had burst open on impact and there were bodies scattered on the ground. As Barney Barnett examined the wreckage, more witnesses arrived. An archaeological research team from the University of Pennsylvania was in the area, excavating sites near Black Mountain and Bat Cave. They, too, had been attracted by the metallic glitter, They, like Barnett, wandered in awed silence around this surrealistic scene.

The bodies resembled humans, but were distinctly different in many ways. The were much smaller, three-and-a-half to four feet long. Their heads were disproportionately large compared to their torsos; they had no hair and their eyes were slanted and spaced wide apart. The creatures' clothing was grey and seemed to be one-piece jumpers with no visible buttons or zippers. They were all dead, and all appeared to be males.

As Barnett and the others were peering timorously into the shattered craft, a military truck drove up. An Air Force officer got out and curtly ordered the civilians to leave the area. He informed them that the crash site was under the jurisdiction of the Air Force, and since matters of national security were involved, they were not to speak about what they had seen.

As the civilians began to leave, more military trucks began to arrive and guards encircled the entire area.

Meanwhile, back on the Foster Ranch, Mac Brazel was swinging down from his saddle, pushing up the curled brim of his hat to survey the damndest mess he'd ever seen in a sheep pasture.

Pieces of whatever had fallen from the sky during the storm were scattered all about. Mac found fragments of light-weight metal he could not bend with his hands. The substance resembled tin foil that he could not tear, and a darker-colored foil which, when he wrinkled it up and lay it back down on the ground, immediately resumed its original shape. Then he found pieces of wood.

The wooden strips looked like balsa, very light and pliable, but unbreakable; Mac's thumbnail didn't even make a dent when he tried to scratch them and, strangest of all, there were colored symbols printed on the wood . . . markings which to Mac made less sense than chicken scratchings.

Mac Brazel picked up a few souvenirs and took them back to the ranch house. That evening, he went to the home of his neighbor, Floyd Foster. The usually taciturn Brazel was very excited, Foster recalled, talking a mile-a-minute about the weird things he'd found that morning. He wanted Foster to come over and see for himself, but Foster, feeling tired, passed up the opportunity of a lifetime.

The next night, July 4, Mac drove into Corona and heard for the first time about the rash of flying saucer reports in the area. He told a couple of friends about his own discovery; they both agreed he ought to report what he had found in Foster's pasture. On July 6, Mac drove into Roswell and talked to the county sheriff.

Sheriff Wilcox immediately called Major Jesse A. Marcel, intelligence officer for the 509th Bomb Group at Roswell Army Air Base. The major's lunch at the officers' club was interrupted by the news from Brazel. Major Marcel quickly contacted the base commander, Colonel William Blanchard. The major was ordered to go back to Brazel's ranch and conduct a thorough investigation.

It was late in the day when Marcel, in his staff car, and a crew of enlisted men in a Jeep Carry-All, finished the bumpy ride to Mac's desert home. In the morning, the entire crew went out to the crash site. What Marcel saw that day must have made up for the discomforts of the night before. Major Marcel had been a pilot since 1928, had flown combat missions in World War II and was present during the Kwajalein atomic bomb tests in 1946 . . . but he was totally unprepared for the pile of litter that had somehow landed in a back-country rancher's sheep pasture.

Years later, after he had retired and perhaps felt he could speak more freely, Marcel said the wreckage was definitely not a plane, a missile, a weather balloon or a radar tracking device. He emphasized that all they found were fragments, but that these bits and pieces were, to him, inexplicable.

Brazel showed the major pieces of the parchment-like fabric and bits of the strange "wood" with symbols painted on it. For lack of a better word, Marcel called the symbols "hieroglyphics"; the pink and purple characters were beyond deciphering.

Major Marcel held his cigarette lighter beneath the wood-like material, but it would not burn. An enlisted man brought him a two-foot long piece of metal that was as thin as a sheet of paper. Marcel watched as the soldier hit it with a hammer and could not dent it.

The major and his crew loaded the debris into the two vehicles, then convinced Mac Brazel that it was his patriotic duty to give up the souvenirs he had collected among the wreckage. With that confiscation completed, the bizarre happening was now neatly concealed from public scrutiny. Everyone had voluntarily agreed to keep quiet about the discoveries, and no physical evidence of the crashes remained at either site.

The whole incident should have become nothing more than a soon-to-be-forgotten rumor. It probably would have faded away without notice except for a young lieutenant named Walter Haut.

Haut was the public information officer at Roswell Army Air Base. On July 8, 1947, he made the biggest mistake of his life, a mistake that would destroy his military career. Haut, recognizing a good story when he heard one, sent out a press release about the amazing finds in the New Mexico desert.

This unauthorized press release, which immediately appeared in newspapers across the country, announced that the Air Force had gained possession of a flying object, a "disc, three feet across" which they were inspecting at the Roswell base.

Needless to say, Haut's superior officers went through the ceiling. Haut was promptly reassigned to another base; he resigned his commission a few months later.

Even so, on July 9, the top brass at Roswell Army Air Base found themselves facing the most dreaded of all peacetime crises... unwanted media attention. They quickly responded with a counter-attack: a press conference. At Fort Worth Army Air Base, where the wreckage had already been flown, General Roger Maxwell Ramey displayed pieces of a weather balloon and its kite to the assembled reporters, allowing the remnants to be photographed. That was all it was, General Ramey said. Just a weather balloon, downed in a storm.

Apparently, none of the newsmen bothered to ask why, if that's all it was, had it been flown on a special plane all the way to Texas. Still the general's explanation was greeted with a fair measure of skepticism.

But the odd discoveries were not over yet. On July 10, Mr. and Mrs. C.B. Brackley of Sweetwater, Texas, were driving east on Highway 70-380 about 14 miles out of Roswell when they saw a flying disc which "rolled over and over" and was in full view for 60 to 75 seconds.

A quick map-check shows this location approximately 10 air-miles southeast of the Brazel and Foster ranches. Could the second disc have been searching for the lost craft?

It is interesting to note that at this time, one week after the crash, it was commonly believed by the media that there was only one crash site. There were rumors about something really weird having come down on the plains of San Augustín, but almost everybody's attention had been diverted by the Roswell incident. The Air

Force had quickly and thoroughly cleaned up the San Augustín site, and all physical evidence, whatever it may have been, was long gone.

Only years later did other witnesses begin to speak up about what they had seen in the days following July 2, 1947. Some people claimed to have personally seen the alien bodies, either at the site, in transit, or at the place they are allegedly stored to this day. In 1979, UFO researchers Charles Berlitz and William L. Moore did an admirable job of tracking down and interviewing many of the witnesses who were still alive 32 years after the incident.

In 1985, an independent researcher, Robert Hastings, used the federal Freedom of Information Act to obtain classified Federal Bureau of Investigation memoranda which he swears will prove that the Air Force recovered not one, but three flying saucers and nine extra-terrestrial bodies, in the New Mexico backcountry between 1947 and 1950.

On the basis of a sizeable accumulation of information, a possible sequence of events can now be constructed.

The plausible scenario begins when something big flew over the Wilmot house in Roswell on the night of July 2, 1947. Within minutes, it was over Mac Brazel's ranch when it was struck by lightning and partially destroyed. The crippled craft made it over the Sierra Oscura range and crashed on the Plains of San Augustín. The debris taken to Roswell was later flown to Fort Worth, Texas, then on to Wright Field in Ohio, while the wreckage and the alien bodies were shipped by rail to Muroc Air Force Base in California. There, autopsies were performed by Borderland Sciences Research Foundation of Vista, California.

Although the whole operation was conducted in utmost secrecy, there were just too many people involved to prevent all leaks. So, from time to time, curious stories have surfaced. The servicemen involved in the transportation, the scientists who examined the materials, and others who had friends with high security clearances began cautiously telling strange tales. Their stories were as fragmented as the saucer itself, but they were hard to dismiss totally.

Then on February 20, 1954, the whole matter took on a new significance when President Dwight D. Eisenhower supposedly made an unpublicized visit to Muroc (now Edwards) Air Force Base. Allegedly, Ike toured the secret facilities containing the wrecked disc and the preserved alien bodies. The president was on one of his frequent golfing vacations in Palm Springs at the time, and when he disappeared for the better part of the day, the press corps raised such a clamor that Press Secretary James Haggerty had to announce that the president had merely gone to the dentist. Haggerty did not mention that Muroc Base had gone on a complete security alert at the same time.

Another interesting anecdote circulated in the early 1960s. U.S. Senator Barry Goldwater reportedly asked General Curtis LeMay for permission to visit the secret facility at Muroc. But General LeMay flatly refused, adding that he himself was forbidden to go in there.

In December 1974, Goldwater confirmed in a letter to Leonard H. Stringfield, public information director for the National Investigations Committee on Aerial Phenomena (NICAP), that he had, indeed, attempted to get permission to see the "UFO information" stored by the Air Force, and that he had been denied access.

For the average American citizen, all this might have been a little far-fetched. New Mexico was an exotic, faraway place anyway, probably full of superstitious, gullible people. Nevertheless, strange events just kept on happening in the Land of Enchantment. If folks weren't impressed with last week's UFO sighting, they could simply wait a few days and there would be a new one to contemplate.

Throughout 1948-49, many documented UFO sightings were made at White Sands Proving Ground where the Skyhook balloon tests were then in progress. On April 5, 1948, a group of scientists watched a disc-shaped object perform high-speed maneuvers for several minutes before it sped out of sight. Not long after them, a pair of circular UFOs rose from near the horizon and circled a balloon that was being tracked by a C-47 plane. When the balloon was retrieved later, it was found to have been torn.

One of the best observations was made April 24, 1949, when a large group of scientists, engineers and technicians released yet another Skyhook balloon. The weather was perfectly clear and there was no wind. When the giant balloon reached 10,000 feet, a silver, oval-shaped object appeared and moved rapidly across the sky. It was studied through a theodolite with a 25-power telescope, and it was timed for six seconds with a stopwatch.

Later, an astrophysicist, Dr. Donald Menzel, would write that these observers had simply seen the refracted images of the balloons themselves, an assertion that enraged members of the Skyhook project. To say they had been fooled by refracted images was tantamount to calling them incompetent.

The real problem was that UFO reports were coming in much faster than plausible explanations would be advanced for them. On April 27, 1950, after a White Sands guided missile test had been completed, a bright object streaked across the night sky. It was photographed by a ground station crew, but the film turned out blurry and dark.

In May, another shiny, aerial object was photographed by two cameras and, although again the footage was of poor quality, the White Sands Data Reduction Group estimated the object was more than 40,000 feet above the earth, traveling over 2,000 miles an hour. They calculated the object to be more than 300 feet in diameter.

Still other reports added to the mounting fascination with UFOs. The sky over Farmington put on a spectacular show during March 1950. For three days, literally hundreds of saucer-shaped discs cavorted in the air above that small town. Nearly everyone in and around Farmington saw them and agreed they were traveling at incredible rates of speed, darting about in crazy flight patterns.

Edward J. Ruppelt, a respected and objective researcher who headed the U.S. Air Force UFO investigation, Project Blue Book, advanced the theory that the "Farmington Fly-by" may have been caused by the fragments of a Skyhook balloon which was known to have burst somewhere in the Four Corners area. He was careful to add, however, that no pieces of the feather-light fabric were ever found.

Explainable or not, UFOs were now being taken very seriously by the United States government, the general public and by the media. By 1952, serious consideration was being given to the establishment of visual spotting stations throughout New Mexico; this state still had the honor of producing more UFO reports than any other.

A tremendous amount of study and research was now bringing forth many reasonable explanations for much of the baffling phenomena. Many sightings were simply the misidentification of conventional aerial objects: balloons, aircraft, planets, searchlights on clouds and even flights of moths. But a disturbingly large percentage of the sightings was still classified as "unknown".

As time went on, things calmed down in New Mexico, with fewer UFO reports made. Sure, there was still the occasional "green fireball" hovering in the mountains and a blinding light or two, but overall, there didn't seem to be much going on . . . until 1964.

In late April of that year, New Mexico was back in the headlines when a story hit the wire services which was so sensational that a small New Mexican town most Americans had never heard of became famous overnight.

HOW TO GET TO THE UFO CRASH SITE

The exact location of the UFO crash site on the San Augustín Plains cannot be pinpointed precisely, but enough data is known to come close.

Drive 109 miles west of Socorro on U.S. Highway 60 to reach the tiny hamlet of Old Horse Springs. Five miles east of Old Horse Springs, a gravel road goes south to the Farr Ranch. Similarly, five miles west of Old Horse Springs, another road runs south to the Y Ranch. Barney Barnett was driving one or the other of those roads when he spotted the wreckage on that summer morning in 1947. He said the crash site was approximately a mile from the road.

Using data from a 1947 map in American Antiquity *magazine we know where the archaeological team that visited the crash site was working. Black Mountain is roughly 14 air-miles southwest of Old Horse Springs, and Bat Cave is about 14 air-miles directly south. This puts the downed saucer within a small rectangular-shaped area circled by the 6750 to 6850 elevation lines in the sections just east of the Second Guide Meridian West and the First Standard Parallel South.*

It has been over 40 years since this mysterious object plunged to earth, but maybe now would be a good time to take a second look at the site. The impact may well have driven fragments of the craft into the ground that were overlooked by the Air Force in 1947. The desert's erosion may have uncovered some of the remaining pieces, or a scan with metal detectors might be productive. Anyone planning to do any real searching should get permission from the local ranchers: G. Farr Ranch, L.B. Moore Ranch and the Y Ranch.

BIBLIOGRAPHY

SPACE TRAVELERS' RENDEZVOUS
Chapter Fifteen

Albuquerque Journal. June, July, 1947; November 12, 1985; June 9, 1986.

Associated Press and International News Service. July 1947.

Berlitz, Charles and Moore, William L. **The Roswell Incident.** New York. Grosset and Dunlap. 1980.

Briazack. Norman J. and Menick, Simon. **The UFO Guidebook.** Secaucus, N.Y. Citadel Press. 1978.

Jacobs, David Michael. **The UFO Controversy in America.** Bloomington, Ind. Indiana University Press. 1972.

Klass, Philip. **UFO's Explained.** New York. Random House. 1974.

Ruppelt, Edward J. **The Report on Unidentified Flying Objects.** Garden City, N.Y. Doubleday. 1956.

16

GALACTIC PIT STOP IN SOCORRO

Socorro, New Mexico, is not exactly the nation's most exciting town. It is one of those places most travelers buzz right on by without a sideward glance as they speed down the interstate highway. Somehow, it never had much to offer that couldn't be found somewhere else further down the road.

In 1964, Socorro had even less than it does today, but it had a certain charm, nonetheless. There was the long main street to cruise, Shirley's Drive-In where one could devour malts and burgers, and the oldtimers certainly found plenty to keep themselves occupied around the town plaza. Socorro always looked content with itself, but it didn't attract too many outsiders. Just about the only travelers who stopped were those who needed a tank of gas or wanted to check under the hood for a worrisome engine knock.

On April 25, 1964, at 5:50 p.m. two very unusual visitors stopped on the outskirts of Socorro. They landed in an arroyo south of town and apparently had a typical tourist problem. They needed to look under the hood. Minutes later, they were gone, but the little town of Socorro wouldn't be quite the same ever again.

Other tourists passed through Socorro on that windy, spring afternoon. A husband and wife with their three youngsters were driving a green 1955 Cadillac with Colorado plates on the highway just south of town when an oval-shaped, metallic object flashed over their car. Whatever it was came in so low it hit the car's radio antenna. The startled family watched as this "new type of aircraft" rapidly descended below their line of vision, into the rough, undeveloped terrain just west of the highway.

Moments later, they saw a white Pontiac police car pull off a street parallel to Highway 85 and bounce down a dirt track toward the spot where they had seen the flying object.

The events that reportedly took place during the next three minutes would later be investigated for months and analyzed down to the fractions of seconds.

Driving the police car was Lonnie Zamora. He is an almost classic example of the ideal, small town law officer: serious, professional and experienced in his work. Zamora is an observant man with quick reactions, a fine eye for detail and excellent recall. No one who knew him well had ever questioned his integrity.

Lonnie Zamora was following a speeding car on the south end of town when he heard a roaring noise and saw a blue flame coming down in the southwest about half a mile away. He knew there was a dynamite storage shed in that area and his first impression was an obvious one: he thought the shed had exploded. He made a quick right turn onto the rough dirt track that led to the shed, spun his tires over the steep, gravelly slope and made it to the top of the low ridge from which he saw a strange, white, metal object in the arroyo below.

At first glance, he thought it was an overturned car. Then he noticed it was oddly shaped, balanced on four leg-like extensions. He also saw two small figures standing near the large object. He said later the figures were wearing clothing similar to white coveralls, and that they appeared quite startled by Zamora's arrival. As the officer drove closer, he radioed the sheriff's office, reporting a possible accident. He requested that State Police Sergeant Samuel Chavez be dispatched to the scene.

Zamora lost sight of the craft momentarily as he crossed a dip in the landscape. When he got back on the ridge, the object was only about 50 feet away, close enough that now he could see a curious red insignia on its side. The two tiny figures were gone. As Zamora braked to a stop and swung out of his car, he heard a heavy slam from the vehicle, like someone closing the hatch of an army tank. There was a second slam from the strange vehicle.

Zamora had run no more than three paces toward the object when a bright blue flame burst from beneath it, discharging a roar so deafening that he instinctively threw himself to the ground.

Recovering somewhat, he ran in a crouch around the back of his car, stumbled, knocked off his glasses and continued running for about 25 feet before looking back. The egg-shaped craft was rising now, and Zamora, expecting an explosion, ran another 25 feet. Then the roar stopped, the flame disappeared and the object began moving away in a straight line.

Officer Zamora dashed back to his car, retrieved his glasses and through the radio tried to describe to the Socorro police dispatcher what he was seeing. After the object had traveled for nearly a mile at a height of about 20 feet, it shot upward and finally disappeared from sight over the mountains to the southwest.

State Police Sergeant Chavez soon arrived on the scene and accompanied the badly-shaken Zamora down into the arroyo where a large greasewood bush was smouldering. They found four depressions in the soil, in a quadrangular pattern, around the bush. The imprints appeared to have been pushed into the ground by an enormous weight.

Other law enforcement officers began to converge, at least two of them promptly enough to observe the smoking bush. Officer Ted Jordan took polaroid photographs of the soil indentations and when the burned area was examined, they noticed that the sand there had been melted into glass.

Back in town, the sheriff's office had received three calls from Socorro residents who had seen a bright blue light in the area south of town. A gas station attendant named Opal Grinder reported a story that had been told to him by an excited Colorado family while he gassed up their green Cadillac.

Nobody on the Socorro police force got much rest that night in April 1964. Agent J. Arthur Byrnes of the Federal Bureau of Investigation was at the police station by 7:00 p.m.; Captain Richard T. Holder, up-range commander at White Sands Missile Range Stallion Site, got there minutes later. They all trooped back to the formerly obscure gully where the downed craft had been seen.

In the morning, the news was officially released to the press; reporters descended on Socorro in droves. By now the site examination had revealed additional imprints in the ground. Four smaller and lighter indentations about four feet from the burned spot and a few tiny "shoeprints" in precisely the same spot Lonnie Zamora said he saw the humanoids standing. Zamora had been able to pinpoint the exact location of the standing figures because they had been silhouetted against a large greasewood bush.

Observers speculated that the four perfectly parallel impressions might have been created when a ladder was lowered from the craft and then repositioned before the aliens descended.

It took a couple of days before America's top UFO experts began to descend on Socorro. First on the scene were James and Carol Lorenzen, both independent civilian researchers who had previously published many carefully documented articles on UFO sightings. They reached Socorro at 2 a.m., April 26; Dr. J. Allen Hynek, an Air Force UFO consultant and professor of astronomy at Northwestern University, got to town early on April 28; Ray Stanford, consultant to Project Blue Book, and a representative for the National Investigations Committee on Aerial Phenomena (NICAP), drove in the same day.

By this time, the Air Force seemed to be firmly but subtly in control of the situation. Lonnie Zamora had been instructed by Captain Holder not to talk anymore about certain aspects of the incident, particularly the curious "insignia" he had seen on the side of the craft.

The Lorenzens toured the site, were briefed by Air Force officials, and may have been misled on several pertinent facts. Allen Hynek, after his initial investigation, taped an interview for KSRC Radio with Major William Connor, a public information officer from Kirtland Air Force Base in Albuquerque, standing at his side. Hynek seemed nervous and uncharacteristically evasive in his statements.

Later, Hynek would inform his own boss, Major Hector Quintanilla, head of Project Blue Book, that he firmly believed Zamora was telling the truth. While he was in Socorro, Hynek remained noncommital about Zamora's story.

Ray Stanford, suspecting a cover-up was in progress, pursued a more independent investigation. He quickly turned up two witnesses who lived near the arroyo and they swore they, too, had heard the roar mentioned by Zamora. Stanford also learned about the vitrified sand at the burned spot, but when he searched the area, it was gone.

Stanford had been accompanied by Hynek, Zamora and Chavez when he first visited the site. They were taking photographs and samples of the burned bush, and some scorched bits of paper when Zamora knelt by the northwest landing gear imprint and pointed out a fractured rock that had obviously been broken when the imprint was made.

Stanford had concealed his excitement during that last discovery, returning to town with the others. Later he hurried back to the site alone. He took photographs of the stone, then bent down in a light misty rain to wrench the rock out of the ground. After wrapping it in newspaper, he carried it up the slope and stashed it under the front seat of his Volkswagen car.

In less than five minutes, Ray Stanford had appropriated the most important piece of physical evidence on the Socorro site, although even he was not yet aware of its full significance. Stanford's memento would eventually suffer the same fate as Mac Brazel's souvenirs at the UFO crash site near Roswell 15 years earlier. But on the morning of April 30, 1964, the fractured stone was on its way to Phoenix as Stanford's little car purred west on Highway 60.

Once home in Phoenix, Stanford carefully unwrapped the stone, held it up in the sunlight and took his first close look at its fractured edge. None of the rest of us who share this planet with Ray Stanford are likely to ever experience the emotional rush he must have felt when he saw what was on the rock.

Small bits of shiny metal, distinct specks and rolled-up slivers had been scraped onto the coarse surface of the stone. They were tiny . . . but they were there.

Stanford called Richard Hall, the NICAP representative in Washington, DC. Hall made arrangements for the stone to be examined at the Goddard Space Flight Center of the U.S. National Aeronautics and Space Administration (NASA). Although he was reluctant to part with this prized possession, Stanford realized that only a facility like Goddard could do a proper analysis of the specks on the rock. He hand-transported the rock in a special carrying case to the Spacecraft Systems Branch of Goddard where the metal particles were removed and subjected to an extensive and lengthy analysis.

A week later, Dr. Henry Frankel, department head of the Spacecraft Systems Branch, informed both Stanford and Hall by telephone that the results of the test were astonishing. The metal was an alloy, primarily zinc and iron, which was not known to be manufactured anywhere in the world.

By divulging this information, Frankel apparently made the same type of mistake that Lieutenant Haut had made in Roswell years before. Within days, Frankel was taken off the Socorro rock sample study, and NASA soon issued a formal document stating the particles on Stanford's stone were nothing more than silica, a very common element.

All of the physical evidence from the Socorro site, what little there had been, was now neatly wrapped up and tucked away; the melted sand was gone, the metallic scrappings had been clumsily but officially discredited. Then, two years later, a UFO-debunker named Phillip J. Klass arrived in Socorro, asked a lot of questions around town and concluded that the actual incident itself had never taken place. The whole thing had been a hoax, Klass wrote, a publicity stunt to attract tourists.

Klass noted that the town had tried to capitalize on the publicity; officials had quickly graded the rutroad past the landing site to make it more accessible to tourists. He found it suspicious that the land was owned by Socorro's mayor. He thought the Colorado Cadillac was pure invention, and he turned up a local resident who lived upwind of the arroyo who said he had not heard the UFO's roar. Though Klass saw only photographs of the burned area, he felt they did not show the kind of severe damage that should have resulted from such a powerful, fiery blast-off. The incident, he said, could have been only one of two things: either it was an actual extra-terrestrial landing or a hoax. He said he was absolutely sure it was the latter.

But Klass's analysis is weak. His hoax theory implies, first of all, that a lot of people were lying; Lonnie Zamora, Samuel Chavez, Opal Grinder, the witnesses who said they heard the roar, the ones who reported seeing the blue flame, and others. Such a hoax would have required a rather sizeable cast of characters.

Even so, how could perpetrators have pulled off such an elaborate scam, step by step? First, they would have had to construct a "landing site". After taking exact and careful measurements, they would have shoveled out landing gear imprints that would appear to have been squeezed into the ground, rather than scooped out. Next, they would press the ladder-foot marks into the soil, not once which seems logical, but twice which makes less sense, and then they would create those tiny footprints off to the side without leaving any of their own. There would be other details to contrive as well, such as the cracked rock, and making sure that all collaborators agreed on the story about the soon-to-vanish patch of melted sand.

While going through this elaborate staging, they would have to hope they wouldn't be seen by passersby on the highway.

After the stage was set, Lonnie Zamora would go into his act, roaring his patrol car over the rough terrain, shouting a rehearsed script into his car radio and then dash down the slope to set fire to the bush. Sam Chavez, on cue, would arrive just in time to see the smouldering remains of Lonnie's bonfire.

All of that would have been the easiest part of the hoax. Much harder would be facing the press, the Air Force, the FBI and the best UFO investigators in the country. The pranksters would have to be interrogated hour after hour, day after day, without making a slip-up. Perhaps hardest of all would be to keep a straight face for the next 20 years, never bursting out in a bar or social setting about the fantastic stunt they'd pulled off.

Was the Socorro landing a hoax? Well, if it was, Lonnie Zamora deserved an Academy Award for Best Actor in 1964.

Hometown boosters have gone to great lengths in New Mexico to attract tourists. But somehow a Duck Race in Deming, or a Ralph Edwards fiesta in Truth or Consequences seem a whole lot easier and more rewarding in the long run than a fake UFO landing.

The Soccoro incident definitely remains an "unknown". It is still the only case of a three-way combination of a reported UFO landing accompanied by physical traces and occupant sightings that is listed in the Project Blue Book files as "unidentified".

HOW TO GET TO SOCORRO'S UFO LANDING SPOT

The town of Socorro has grown somewhat since 1964. Now several businesses and dwellings flank the "landing site". The site itself, however, remains just as it was—open, rough and brushy.

It can be visited from the junction of U.S. Highway 85 and Highway 1 at the south end of Socorro's main street. Take Highway 1 a short distance to the Socorro RV Park. Turn right at the north end of the park and circle around behind it on a narrow, paved road. The terrain on your right is the area where the UFO touched down.

Now, watch for a sign pointing the way to the Socorro Baptist Temple. Drive this rocky, washboard track west to a rise in the land just above the church. From there, you can visually trace the saucer's take-off flight path.

To the southwest, you will see a two-peak, mining-scarrred hill with a perlite mill at the base of the hill. The UFO passed directly over the mill before it shot straight up between the two peaks and vanished.

BIBLIOGRAPHY

GALACTIC PITSTOP IN SOCORRO
Chapter Sixteen

Albuquerque Journal, April, May, 1964.

Briazack, Norman J. and Menick, Simon. **The UFO Guidebook.** Secaucus, N.Y. Citadel Press. 1978.

Jacobs, David Michael. **The UFO Controversy in America.** Bloomington, Ind. Indiana University Press. 1972.

Klass, Philip. **UFO's Explained.** New York. Random House. 1974.

Ruppelt, Edward J. **The Report on Unidentified Flying Objects.** Garden City, N.Y. Doubleday. 1956.

Stanford, Ray. **Socorro Saucer in a Pentagon Pantry.** Austin, Tex. Blueapple Books. 1976.

17

BIZARRE CATTLE
MUTILATIONS

The night sky of New Mexico is a vast panorama of stars. Out in the desert or on the lonely rangelands and high country pastures, far from the glare of city lights, the stars always seem brighter and closer. The moon appears larger. The darkness blacker.

But for ranchers living in these sparsely populated areas, the night sky holds an ominous fascination. It can be a thing of both beauty and dread. Ranchers suffering from a special plague believe, from their own personal experience, that there is something else out there besides stars in the deep, black void.

During the early 1970s, remote ranchers of New Mexico began experiencing a series of bizarre and unexplainable cattle mutilations. The pattern was always the same; the animals had been killed at night and their sexual organs, rectums and udders appeared to have been removed with very sharp instruments. Often, the lips, tongue and eyes had also been cut out and the carcass was drained of blood. No footprints or tire-tracks were found near the mutilated animals, but sometimes a circular indentation surrounded the body along with tripod-like tracks, 14 inches in diameter. Reports of strange, unidentified aircraft frequently accompanied the discovery of the mutilated livestock.

On July 3, 1978 in the village of Ranchitos in northern New Mexico where many of the mutilations have occurred, Mrs. Elias Vargas was awakened by a crackling noise and a bright orange light that lit up her bedroom. From her window, she saw a round, glowing form twice the size of an automobile hovering near the house. The object's color changed from orange to grey, she said, before it suddenly sped away and disappeared in a matter of seconds.

On the night of April 9, 1979, two Jicarilla Apache tribal police officers were making a routine patrol of cattle herds in the reservation backcountry. At 2:10 a.m., they were driving with the vehicle lights off when they spotted an unidentifiable aircraft poised about 50 feet above the ground, aiming a powerful spotlight at a herd of cattle. The Apache officers initiated radio contact with the New Mexico State Police, through Patrolman Gabe Valdéz who was patroling nearby.

When the two officers turned on their car headlights, the aircraft instantly shut off its spotlight and rose swiftly to fly south. State Policeman Valdéz was four miles away when he received the sighting report. He said the aircraft flew over him, but he could not see it clearly in the darkness, and could hear no sound as it went past.

Four hundred miles to the north, the Air Traffic Control Center in Longmont, Colorado, picked up the aircraft on its radar screen, flying at an altitude of 5,800 feet, at a speed of 300 miles an hour. The radar blip was lost about 20 miles north of Albuquerque.

Strange as these sightings were, they had long since ceased being unique. Over a ten-year period, literally thousands of cattle and horses had been killed and systematically mutilated within a 15-state area. The economic loss to ranchers was estimated to be $2.5 million nationwide. The perpetrators of these mysterious crimes had operated with unprecedented discipline; although the crimes had been extensively investigated, not one solid clue had been produced as to identity or motivation.

In 1976, a newly-elected United States Senator, Harrison "Jack" Schmitt of New Mexico, found himself besieged with requests from rancher constituents seeking federal help in solving these frightening crimes. Schmitt was immediately intrigued by the problem. He seemed a natural, almost ironically appropriate, choice to head up a federal probe. Schmitt was a former U.S. astronaut, one of the few human beings who has actually been out into that black night sky far beyond the earth.

After consultations with U.S. Attorney General Griffin Bell, Schmitt determined there was sufficient cause for a federal investigation. Since many of the mutilations had taken place on Indian reservations, and had apparently involved the use of unmarked aircraft, federal laws apparently had been violated. On this basis, the Justice Department began considering intervention by the Federal Bureau of Investigation.

On April 20, 1979, Senator Schmitt, a geologist by profession, organized and chaired the nation's first National Cattle Mutilation Conference in Albuquerque. "There are few activities more dangerous than an unsolved pattern of crimes," the senator said. "It is time to get as many knowledgeable people together as possible."

Schmitt's conference succeeded admirably in that respect; it drew an incredibly diverse group of witnesses. In the hushed atmosphere of the lower-level auditorium of the Albuquerque Main Library, dark-suited FBI agents mingled with ranchers in faded Levis. Pueblo Indians wearing turquoise, uniformed State Police officers, bearded UFO buffs and space age scientists stepped to the microphones one after the other to address what they knew or suspected.

"The only thing that makes sense about the mutilations is that they make no sense at all," said David Perkins, director of Colorado's Animal Mutilation Probe. Perkin's group had been systematically collecting data since 1975. He displayed a heavily-pinned map of cattle mutilation sites and noted that placement of the mutilations indicated inexplicable concentrations and timings.

Perkins made no attempt to hide his belief that the mutilations were caused by extra-terrestrial visitors. His tone of voice changed dramatically as he said, "This may be the biggest challenge mankind has ever faced. It may prove everything we believe is wrong. The answer may have something to do with our survival on this planet."

Rancher Manuél Gomez was somewhat more down to earth. Gomez's weathered face attested to his 30 years as a New Mexico cattleman; he looked like a man who has endured many hardships. He held the dubious distinction of being the rancher in Rio Arriba County hardest hit by the mutilators. Over the three previous years, he had lost six expensive cattle in the same grisly fashion.

This loss had not cost him his sense of humor, however. He referred to the mutilations as "Cattlegate" and chuckled as he said, "Maybe they're making push-button cows nowadays. When they lay on their right side, all their organs pop out and their blood evaporates."

A veterinarian from Los Alamos, Dr. Richard Prine, viewed the entire proceedings with unconcealed contempt. He testified to having examined several carcasses and found nothing unusual. "Animals are the source," he said. "It is simply the work of ordinary predators."

Later, State Police Officer Gabe Valdéz stepped to the podium and directly contradicted Prine's remarks. Valdéz is a highly respected law officer in northern New Mexico. There was a light ripple of applause as he took the stage. Over a period of several years, Valdéz had investigated more than 30 cattle mutilations.

"If this is the work of predators," he said, "then we must have predators with super powers. What kind of predator can take the entire heart of a cow out through a small hole in the neck?"

Dr. Claire Hibbs, of the state diagnostic laboratory at New Mexico State University, verified Valdéz's testimony. He placed cattle mutilations in three categories. The majority of reports can be dismissed as livestock deaths from natural causes followed by coyote and scavenger attacks on the carcasses. The second and smallest category is that of pranksters ... dead cows that have been clumsily mutilated by local practical jokers.

The third category is the unexplainable: cattle whose organs have apparently been severed by knives or sharp instruments with almost surgical precision.

Senator Schmitt added that most of the mutilations are reported to have occurred in the early morning hours, usually around 4:00 a.m., and are often accompanied by the sounds and sightings of "helicopters". The senator related an incident reported to him by a constituent in southeastern New Mexico. The rancher had heard the sound of helicopters in the night and had discovered a calf missing in the morning. He found evidence that the calf had been dragged to the fence line and from there had disappeared. "So far as I know," said Senator Schmitt, "that calf has never been found."

Stranger still was the testimony given by Tommy Blann who had spent the past 12 years studying animal mutilations in depth. Blann told of finding cattle whose heads had been twisted 360 degrees and whose bodies lay within disturbed circles where the shrubs and rocks had literally been rotated into the ground.

Blann noted that many of the cattle were found to have broken bones and crushed rib cages. "Some of them have definitely been dropped." His research had taken him all the way to the British Museum in London where he found records of cattle mutilations that occurred in England and Scotland nearly 200 years ago. He noted that Sir Arthur Conan Doyle once investigated a series of animal mutilations for which he could find no explanation.

"This problem is international in scope," Blann said. "Mutilations have been reported in Pakistan, Australia, South Wales, Sweden and Canada."

Reports from far-off lands and faded documents in dusty archives are of little importance to the average hard-working New Mexico rancher. Raliegh Tafoya, governor of the Jicarilla Apache Tribe, was more concerned about the three cattle he himself had lost to mutilators.

"I don't believe in the UFO," he said, "because I have never seen it myself. Others say they have seen it, but I have not. Still we know these things have happened. And I wonder if the lives of human beings will be next."

Then, enigmatically, he added: "We know that threats have been made."

Senator Schmitt immediately grasped the microphone to demand, "If you know of threats, Mr. Tafoya, we want to hear about them."

Raliegh Tafoya hesitated momentarily; then he left the stage without further comment.

Reticence on the part of Native Americans to discuss livestock mutilations on their lands was emphasized in later testimony. Reports from Sandia Laboratories in Albuquerque show that Indians had frequently refused to allow investigators on their property after mutilations occurred. According to a member of the Sandia Labs team, the Indians said the mutilations are "being done by the star people. They are doing it for their own purposes. They must be left alone."

One of the final speakers at the conference in Albuquerque was Dr. Richard Sigismund, a UFO researcher from Boulder, Colorado. Dr. Sigismund is an imposing man with a mane-like beard and intense eyes. He spoke rapidly as if he was trying to convey an urgent message as quickly as possible.

"UFO phenomena is usually heavily reported in connection with cattle mutilations," Dr. Sigismund said. "Though we cannot prove a direct link, the evidence cannot be ignored. Cattle mutilations cannot be blamed on cultists or coyotes. Airborne vehicles are involved; it is an aerial phenomenon."

Sigismund asked the audience to speculate for a moment on all possible causes of livestock mutilations. He noted that many people insist that this is the work of a government agency . . . part of a sinister, secret project. Proponents of this theory argue that the equipment necessary to conduct a project of this scope is far beyond the means of private citizens.

"This argument is untenable," Sigismund added. "Any government agency which left butchered carcasses behind would know that eventually there would be a public outcry and an investigation resulting in exposure of the project."

Sigismund also dismissed a second theory: rituals by cultists. If the mutilations are being carried out by a secret cult, this implies a nationwide organization, lavishly funded and staffed by people with scientific expertise.

Most mutilations are obviously the work of predators and can be easily identified as such, he said. As to the rest of the cases, Sigismund concluded that only one other explanation remains. "We are forced to hypothesize that these occurrences are part of the general category of UFO phenomena."

No one present at the conference could contradict Richard Sigismund's conclusions, and the question of the mutilators' motivation remained the most elusive of all. Howard Burgess, a retired scientist from Sandia Labs, cautiously advanced the theory that since the lips, tongues and rectums are removed from the cattle, the mutilations may be related to a scientific study of the lymphatic system and production of bacteria.

Are the mutilations part of an extra-terrestrial monitoring program? If so, why?

As a result of Senator Schmitt's conference, a task force was formed to thoroughly and scientifically investigate the strange "unsolved pattern of crimes". Santa Fe District Attorney Eloy Martinez applied for and received a $44,170 grant from the Law Enforcement Assistance Administration (LEAA) of the U.S. Department of Justice for the project. On April 26, 1979, Martinez assigned a former FBI agent, Kenneth M. Rommel, to the case.

Rommel had been an FBI agent for 28 years, working primarily on investigations of bank robberies and counter-espionage. The cattle mutilation probe was to be his last assignment; he planned to retire from law enforcement work after the case was closed. Rommel said he was drawn to his final job "partially by the intrigue that has gone with it." He felt this investigation was a fitting climax to his long career.

He did not, however, express much confidence in his ability to solve the mystery. "I hope we will be able to get successful prosecutions," Rommel said, "but if we can't come to a logical conclusion, there will at least be a central repository of information." He then began work on a 14-month investigation.

FBI Agent Rommel made on-site examinations of the mutilations that occurred during those 14 months, received reports and information from other states, and conferred with many knowledgeable veterinarians. In early July 1980, he released a 297-page report which concluded that all of the evidence he had examined and all of the reports and photographs he had received led to only one conclusion: the "so-called mutilations" were nothing more than the work of ordinary predators and animal scavengers.

His report pointed out that scavengers can make cuts, bite wounds and incisions that "to the uninitiated" appear to have been done with surgical precision. In regard to the carcasses that had seemed to be drained of blood, he offered a natural explanation: when a heart stops pumping, the blood is drawn by gravity to the lowest point of the body, leaving the upper portion almost dry.

The parts of the animals' bodies that had been removed were invaribaly the most prominent, accessible and easily chewed, always the inevitable first choice of any hungry coyote, bobcat or bear that happens upon a free dinner in a backcountry pasture.

But during his investigation, Rommel encountered no "classic" mutilations, and concluded that the reports of unidentified aircraft and strange ground impressions surrounding dead livestock were the product of "mildly hysterical" imaginations. He felt the incidents had been blown out of proportion by a sensation-seeking press and had been nurtured by a gullible public's willful suspension of disbelief. He also acknowledged that his conclusions would not be accepted by everyone who read his report.

One person who is definitely in agreement with Rommel is Melecio Sedillo, a careful and thorough investigator for the New Mexico Livestock Board. Over the years, Sedillo had investigated numerous mutilations. Although he found two or three cases he was not sure about, he is nonetheless totally convinced that predators are the culprits in the mystery. He can give almost clinical descriptions of the natural process that takes place after an animal dies on the range.

Predators, usually coyotes, quickly arrive on the death scene and immedately eat the softest parts of the carcass. Soon the body bloats and swells, stretching the incision in a near-perfect circle that appears to have been sliced by a skillfully applied scalpel. The swelling often causes the animal's tongue to protrude from its mouth and the coyotes eat this exposed part. When the swelling subsides, the remainder of the tongue retracts so that when the jaw is pried open, it appears that the tongue had been cut out earlier.

In cases in which an eye had been removed, Sedillo noticed it was always the eye on the exposed side of the head, while the eye on the ground side was still intact. It was obviously predation by birds, such as magpies or crows, he said, adding that he had almost always found animal tracks and bird droppings around the carcasses.

One dead cow that Sedillo examined near Wagon Mound puzzled him for awhile. Its genitals were unmolested, but there was a perfect circle cut out of its stomach. Though he could not be sure, he suspected that the unfortunate animal may have been suffering from water-belly, causing a softening of the hide over the stomach, thus making that area more attractive to predators. Two other cases were sufficiently perplexing that he ordered the carcasses taken to Los Alamos National Laboratories for examination. The lab reports concluded that one of these mutilation cases was predator-caused, while the other may have been done with a sharp instrument.

Like Rommel, Sedillo has never run across a "classic" mutilation and he, too, is aware that not everyone agrees with his conclusions.

One person who has reason to doubt the official explanation is Manuél Gomez, the Rio Arriba County rancher who, prior to the Rommel probe, had lost six cows. During the next four years, he lost four more. The tenth case was the strangest.

On the morning of March 29, 1983, Gomez found another of his cows dead out behind his house near the family cemetery. He called in State Patrolman Gabe Valdéz and together they examined the carcass. The animal appeared to have died the night before and only the udder was gone. But this time, the incised area was different; there was a scalloped effect on the edge of the wound, as if some sort of large pinking shears had been used. The cow's back was broken and it had bruises around three of its legs, indicating it might have been dragged.

That summer, four more cattle mutilations were reported in northern New Mexico, while three took place over the state line in Colorado. A helicopter sighting was reported in conjunction with one of the Colorado incidents. During 1984, no mutilations were reported in New Mexico.

It is also possible, of course, that many ranchers—now believing that the mutilations were caused by predators—no longer bothered to report new incidents. Still, two cases were reported in Colorado in 1984; the second of the two was definitely of a "classic" nature.

It happened on a ranch northeast of Trinidad, 20 miles northeast of New Mexico's Raton Pass. The ranch is owned by Myron Scott, who, on Friday afternoon, October 19, 1984, drove a small herd of cattle into one of his pastures about two miles from his mobile home. That evening after dark, he was feeding his horses when he turned and saw two bright lights in the night sky above the distant pasture. They seemed to be about 100 feet above the ground, no more than four feet apart. Although they were stationary, they were pulsating simultaneously. Scott called his wife, Kathie, to the kitchen window from which she, also, saw the strange lights over the pasture.

One mile north, at the home of Myron Scott's mother, the dogs began to bark uncontrollably. Mrs. Scott switched on the yard light and peered out her back door. She neither saw nor heard anything unusual, but when she tried to hush the dogs, they uncharacteristically refused to obey and kept barking crazily for another 15 minutes.

It was not until late the following Monday afternoon, nearly three days later, that Scott rode out to round up the cattle. He found the herd nervous and skittish, running away as he approached. Then, he found the dead one.

It has been mutilated hideously. The left jaw was peeled clean down to the bone and the tongue had been cut out. The stomach, genitals and intestines were gone and most shocking of all, the hide had been rolled off, the way someone would open a can of sardines.

Scott called the Los Alamos County Sheriff's Office. In the morning, Deputy Carl Veltri and Lou Girodo from the local district attorney's office, went out to take a look at the dead cow. Their examination showed that the horns were loose and wobbly, and the hair around them was rubbed off. Girodo checked the body with a Geiger counter and picked up a slight reading around the head. Next, the investigators made a careful ground search.

They easily picked up Myron Scott's footprints and found a circle of coyote tracks about 20 feet away. There were no other imprints on the ground but there was a trail of dried blood leading out from the head for about 15 feet.

The following morning, Girodo brought a local veterinarian, Dr. William Aaroe, to the scene. The vet agreed that the loose horns and rubbed-off hair indicated that a rope or a cable had been looped around the horns in order to drag the carcass.

But, he also said it was absolutely clear the animal had not been dragged.

The earth around the carcass was undisturbed and there was no dirt, gravel or plant growth stuck in the cow's hair. There were no wear marks on the legs nor scratch marks on the hooves. When Girodo asked Dr. Aaroe if the 800-pound animal might have been lifted up and dropped, the doctor nodded. That, he said, seemed to be the only possible explanation.

Lou Girodo and Kenneth Rommel are at exact opposites in their beliefs about the causes of the mysterious cattle mutilations. Rommel, in his report, wrote that only after predators have been ruled out could other theories be considered, while Girodo says that only after it is proven that "space ships" are not involved can predators receive the entire blame.

Similarly, Melecio Sedillo and Officer Gabe Valdéz are at odds on the issue. "Gabe and I are good friends," said Sedillo. "We've worked together on a lot of mutilation cases, and Gabe's been on several that I haven't. We've talked about it over a couple of beers more than once, but we still totally disagree. Gabe really believes there's something going on out there."

What that "something" actually is may be far beyond the comprehension of anyone here on earth today, but we have no shortage of theories to consider. Thomas Adams, a Texas-based researcher who has collected cattle mutilation evidence since 1978, has examined all the theories concocted over the years and continues to keep an open, but probing, mind toward them all.

Adams notes that the "cult" theory still persists. Somewhere, there is a well-funded secret society or paramilitary organization conducting bizarre research. Or maybe it's the government conducting a massive biological warfare experiment. Perhaps the government is acting in collusion with the extra-terrestrials and they are exchanging data. Or maybe, the extra-terrestrials are doing it completely on their own.

Adams takes no sides, but he believes we should not ignore recent findings which show that many groups of cattle chromosomes are identical to large regions of human chromosomes, and that artificial human blood and hemoglobin solutions can now be produced from cattle blood.

On the other hand, neither can we ignore old Don Coyote.

After all, he's been around a lot longer than any of the rest of us. In legend, Coyote was the first wingless creature to fly to the top of Enchanted Mesa and he's been a fascinating nuisance ever since the first human threw a rock at him.

Coyote has always seemed to be the wisest and wiliest, most cunning and crafty member of the animal kingdom. He has survived all attempts to exterminate him; he seems to cleverly adapt to any and all threats to the well being of his species. Coyote is a near-cosmic animal . . . he's not called "God's Dog" for nothing.

Ranchers report that coyotes will often circle dead livestock at a distance and refuse to move in if they instinctively perceive that something is not quite normal. On other occasions, they unhesitatingly rush in for an instant feast.

"They're smart," said Melecio Sedillo. "Coyotes usually won't go near anything with a human smell around it. But other times they will, if they feel it's safe, or if they're hungry enough."

Gabe Valdéz has witnessed coyotes that circled mutilated animals from 20 feet out, but refused to come any closer. Other investigators have staked out unmutilated carcasses and watched from a distance as the predators raced in to chow down.

Perhaps Old Coyote has a sixth sense, a built-in Geiger counter more sensitive than any we could build. Thomas Adams notes that recent tests show that rats may be able to detect X-rays. So, if a common rat is that sensitive, what level may Coyote have reached?

Coyote has received the official blame for the cattle mutilation mystery. He probably smugly enjoys the notoriety. But he may know a lot more than he's letting on.

Coyote is to the New Mexico backcountry what The Shadow was to old-time radio: he knows where the secrets lurk. He knows he lives in an Enchanted Land where strange and mysterious occurrences are commonplace. He prowls the country by night, so he's probably seen more cattle mutilations, UFOs, ghosts and devils than any of us can imagine. He may have watched Zakyneros carve that Mystery Rock, and witnessed Ah-chi-te climb Enchanted Mesa; he may have been there when the Stone Lion was first placed on the mesa in the Jemez Mountains.

Just as Nature, they say, abhors a vacuum, humans cannot abide unsolved mysteries. How fitting, then, that the irascible, unbeatable Coyote should be blamed for the nagging mystery of New Mexico's cattle mutilations.

HOW TO GET TO AN AREA OF CATTLE MUTILATIONS

None of the carcasses mutilated under mysterious conditions is known to have been preserved. Similarly, there is no specific mutilation site which attracts the curious. In recent years, however, the greatest concentrations of such reported incidents seem to be in northern New Mexico on and around the Jicarilla Apache Reservation. To visit the territory most plagued by the cattle mutilations, drive northwest from Bernalillo on Highway 44 toward Farmington. Shortly after entering the Jicarilla Reservation, about 17 miles past the town of Cuba, take Highway 537 north through the reservation, arriving at the tribal capital, Dulce, after 67 miles.

Mutilated cattle, some in the "classic" fashion, have been found throughout this area during the 1970s and 1980s.

BIBLIOGRAPHY

BIZARRE CATTLE MUTILATIONS
Chapter Seventeen

Adams, Thomas. **Stigmata: The Project Stigma Report.** Paris, Tex. 1985,1986.
Albuquerque Journal. July 9,1980, December 29, 1985.
Interview with Melecio Sedillo. 1986.
Rio Grande Sun. Española, N.M. April 28, 1983; June 23, 1983.
Testimony in Senator Harrison Schmitt's National Cattle Mutilation Conference. Albuquerque, N.M. April 20, 1979.